God's
Promises
for your Children

PRAYER DEVOTIONAL

MIKE SHREVE

ISBN: 978-0-942507-05-8

God's Promises for your Children

Copyright © 2008 Mike Shreve

Library of Congress Control Number: 2008924993
Publisher's Cataloging-in-Publication
(Provided by Quality Books, Inc.)

Shreve, Mike.
God's promises for your children: prayer devotional
/ Mike Shreve.
p. cm.
Includes bibliographical references and index.
ISBN-13: 978-0-942507-05-8
ISBN-10: 0-942507-05-3

1. God—Promises—Biblical teaching. 2. Christian life. 3. Children—Religious life. 4. Parent and child. I. Title.
BT180.P7S55 2008   231.7
                        QBI08-806

My deepest appreciation to the following persons: Layout and Typesetting: Sue Lofton; Proofreaders: Gary Pollard, Jeanne Obee, Winnie Shreve; Cover design: Lonzo Kirkland.

Deeper Revelation Books

Revealing "the deep things of God" (1 Cor. 2:10)
P.O. Box 4260 • Cleveland, TN 37320
Phone: 423-478-2843 • Fax: 423-479-2980
Printed in the United States of America
First Printing-June, 2008—Second Printing-November, 2008

$\underline{12-30-08}$

(Date)

This book is dedicated to:

Kimberly De Four

my lonely daughter

_____

_____

(Name of child or names of children being dedicated)

❧

May the Everlasting God watch over these

promises to fulfill them in your life!

Your mom (MrS Michel)

_____

_____

_____

(Names of parents, grandparents, guardians or intercessors)

Dedication

We dedicate this book to our children: Zion Seth and Destiny Hope. We love you more than we can say in words. Being a father and mother to you actually awakened this truth within our hearts. Not only do we dedicate this book to you, more importantly, we pray and confess that EVERY promise will be fulfilled in your lives.

Mike and Elizabeth Shreve

Zion Seth & Destiny Hope

Table of Contents

PART ONE

A Miracle For Your Family

PART TWO

The Promises

PART THREE

Final Thoughts

PART FOUR

Praise & Progress Journal

Mike, Elizabeth, Destiny and Seth Shreve

Introduction

MIKE SHREVE

As you can easily assume from this recent picture, we are blessed with two healthy, bright, wonderful children. They are both miracles. Our son had a very traumatic birth that should have damaged him irreparably and the prognosis over our daughter, prior to birth, was very dark. Praise God! Prayer works and God had the last word. Against all odds in the natural, they survived. Did this happen because they have Christian parents who are devoted to God—who seek God consistently—who trust God to fulfill His promises? Quite likely! In fact, we would dare to say, "Faith in God had a great deal to do with it!"

At the time of this writing, our son, Zion Seth, is sixteen and our daughter, Destiny Hope, is seven. They're good kids. They do well in school. They love God. But there are still plenty of challenges we face as parents. The fight of faith is not over and we still find ourselves grasping for promises in God's Word that relate to our day-to-day circumstances. Yes, the Bible is still an "anchor of the soul"—not only in the major storms of life, but also in the unanticipated "gusty winds" of minor problems and conflicts (Hebrews 6:19).

Getting acquainted with God's Word is like putting up storm windows and storm doors on our homes, in a spiritual sense. God warned, "My people are destroyed for lack of knowledge" (Hosea 4:6). How often this proves to be true! If we, as parents, do not know what God has said concerning our children, we have no basis for our faith. Then when the wind starts blowing, we're vulnerable—the glass shatters, the doors blow open—and life can get really chaotic.

You may feel you're at a point like that right now. You might even be tempted to give up on parenthood, give up on your children and throw in the towel. Don't do it. Grab that towel. Dry your tears. Refocus. Get adamant. Reclaim your seed.

As Moses informed Pharaoh that they would not go into the wilderness to worship without their children, so you need to inform the prince of darkness, "My children are going with me! You can't have them! I'm not leaving them behind! As for me and my house, we will serve the LORD!"

Do you feel a surge of spiritual adrenalin, just by thinking thoughts of determination like that? Go ahead. The victory is in sight. Eat this book. Digest it. Let it become a part of you. Learn God's promises concerning the offspring of the righteous. Then, start fighting the good fight of faith over your seed. YOU CAN DO IT!

Introduction

I remember waiting with anticipation as I stared down at that little white strip, hoping and praying that this time it would be a bright blue line and not another pink one. From the moment of faint blue turning to bright blue, my heart was filled with both excitement and fear. As the days progressed, I must admit, fear took the lead. Apprehension filled me with questions—"Can I handle the responsibility? Can I do it right? Can I be a good mother?"

It's been fifteen years now, and I wish I could say, "I know all about parenting." I've read a lot of books, ordered all the magazines, even attended parenting classes. All these things have been a great blessing. But these aids alone are not enough. There have been days of great joy and days of great tears. One thing is certain to me; the greatest parenting tool is the Word of God! It has always been my sustaining force.

My pregnancy with Seth, my firstborn, was extremely taxing on my body. I was still in my "Wonder Woman" phase. You know the type, "I can do it all. I can have my cake and eat it too. I can stay on the road and travel with Mike, just like before." We were preaching continuously, running an office and managing a household. Needless to say, I was exhausted.

My "Wonder Woman" phase soon turned into just my "wonder" phase. I *wondered*, "How on earth can I do all of this?" While in prayer, the Word of the LORD came and spoke Psalm 27:13 to my tired soul: "I would have fainted had I not believed to see the goodness of the LORD in the land of the living." Praise God! It was God's goodness that caused me not to faint. I gave birth to a wonderful son. He has been goodness to me. He is intelligent and witty. His future is so bright in God. Yes, the Word of the LORD is my sustaining force.

With Destiny, it was totally different. It wasn't my body in jeopardy; it was the baby. From the beginning, we lived with negative reports. It was always something new. This was wrong and that was wrong (Spinal Bifoda, Cretinism). She would never be normal. She would probably never speak or walk. At one point, one doctor even suggested an "alternative" (we never returned to that office). Once again I turned to my sustaining force. After months of warring against worry and dread, I fixed my focus on the thing that gives life—the Word of God. I began to quote Psalm 138:8 often:

"The LORD will perfect that which concerns me."

I started laying hands on my belly, saying, "You are perfect, little girl. The Word of God says you are perfect. You *concern* me— therefore you are *perfect*." Praise God! When she came out of the womb, the first words the doctor said were, "She's perfect"—and she was. Not only that, she has expressed herself as a real lover of God and worshipper of God at an early age. Praise the LORD for His goodness and perfection! It is the Word that brings forth the miraculous. Hold it close at night! State it! Quote it! Believe it!

These difficult beginning steps in the drama of parenthood taught me a valuable lesson that has remained with me until this day. If we can successfully speak goodness and perfection over our children in natural things, then we can speak goodness and perfection over them in spiritual things as well. This wonderful book will empower you to do that very thing.

PART ONE

A Miracle for Your Family

"Where there is great love, there are always miracles."
—WILLA CATHER

Miracle:
*An extraordinary event manifesting divine
intervention in human affairs.*

God's View of Parenthood

"No job can compete with the responsibility of shaping and molding a new human being." —Dr. James Dobson

You are about to get acquainted with a heart-warming, full-of-hope subject in God's Word: the revelation of 65 promises God has given concerning the offspring of His people. Before we explore these promises, though, we need to lay a good foundation—first, understanding parenthood from God's perspective.

Amazingly, the first sign of the blessing of God, on both animals and men, was procreative power: the ability to bring forth image-bearing offspring. Immediately after creating the animals—

God blessed them, saying, "Be fruitful and multiply."
(Genesis 1:22)

After creating Adam and Eve, God made a similar statement, but with significant additions:

And God blessed them. And God said to them, "Be fruitful, and multiply and fill the earth, and subdue it. And have dominion over the fish of the sea and over the fowl of the heavens, and all animals that move upon the earth."
(Genesis 1:28 MKJV)

Not only did God manifest His blessing upon the foreparents of the human race by empowering them to have children; He revealed His intention to use those children in furthering His purposes in the world. God's aim is still the same. He is determined to fill the earth with righteous, God-loving children. Their task is to carry on the legacy of godly parents by "subduing" the evil here, taking "dominion" over spiritual darkness in the name of the LORD.

Stable homes and stable marriages are far more capable of consistently fulfilling this divine desire. In Malachi 2:15, God commands faithfulness in marriage. Then He explains the reason behind the mandate. He is seeking a "godly seed" (KJV). When infidelity rules a home, it can have a damaging and contaminating effect on children—pushing them toward similar ungodly patterns of living. The Contemporary English Version of this passage says it well:

> *Didn't God create you to become like one person with your wife? And why did he do this? It was so you would have children, and then lead them to become God's people. Don't ever be unfaithful to your wife.* (Malachi 2:15 CEV)

So let it be emphasized, God is seeking children with strong value systems, children who will perpetuate His righteous purposes in the earth, children who will "become God's people." This is high on God's list of priorities, because we don't live on forever, physically speaking. Whatever ground is gained for Christianity in one generation can be totally lost in the next, if the former generation fails to impart passion for the things of God. So parenthood is a great blessing—not only to us, but to God as well—because through our children the hope of God's Kingdom dominating the planet can live on, growing and advancing with each generation.

"When God chose to create man in His own image, He created a marriage, a family. The community of the family is a reflection of the community in the Godhead [the Father, Son and Holy Spirit]. Its identity, life, and power come from God." (Eph. 3:14-15)[†]

[†]*Spirit Filled Life Bible*, (Thomas Nelson Publishers, Nashville, Tennessee, 1991) p.6, bracketed statement inserted by author.

Our View of Parenthood

"The Hebrew word for parents is horim, and it comes from the same root as moreh, teacher. The parent is, and remains, the first and most important teacher that the child will ever have." —Rabbi Kassel Abelson

Recently I saw a somewhat harried woman walking through a discount store with a flock of kids. Her t-shirt read, "Who are these children and why are they calling me 'Mom'?" Maybe you're in a similar agitated state of mind. But living in denial won't help. Come to grips with it—you are a parent. But how do you view this role? Do you look at it as a burden, one more responsibility to fulfill or just a necessary part of life? No, it is much more! A wonderful insight comes from Solomon, the wisdom writer:

Children are an inheritance from the LORD. They are a reward from Him. (Psalms 127:3 GW)

In other words, children are one of God's most wonderful gifts to you; the fruit of the womb is an incomparable and generous legacy from on high. When tough times come and offspring are not as manageable as you would prefer, you might be tempted to say things quite opposite to the passage just quoted. But winning the battles of life—and the challenges of parenting—starts with a choice. You choose to view parenting as God views parenting, and you choose to believe—enough to utter confessions of faith, instead of declarations of doubt.

Speaking negatively over your children is actually a way of "cursing" them. Your words "nudge" them (sometimes "shove" them) toward the very dark, future scenario that you predict. Don't do it!

Even if your kids are stubborn and disrespectful, don't reinforce the negative by making statements like the following:

- *"My children stress me out."*
- *"My children are so rebellious."*
- *"My children just don't respect me."*
- *"My children are walking in darkness."*
- *"My children are in the hands of the enemy."*
- *"My children will never make it in life."*
- *"My children are caught in the world's web."*
- *"I'll be glad when they're out of the nest!"*

Parents who repeatedly say, or even repeatedly think these things, tend to weave a very dark, threefold cord around their own hearts—of doubt, despair and anger. Rid yourself of these binding attitudes right now and weave the opposite. As Zig Zigler suggested, "When you put faith, hope and love together, you can raise positive kids in a negative world." Start by being very positive yourself, and by boldly confessing:

- *"My children are an inheritance from God!"*
- *"My children are part of the fruit I bear in life!"*
- *"My children are a reward from God!"*
- *"My children are a blessing!"*
- *"My children will walk in the light!"*
- *"My children are in the hands of God!"*
- *"My children will fulfill their destiny!"*
- *"My children will be used by God to change this world."*
- *"My children and I are building a relationship with permanent value!"*

Parents cannot voice proclamations like this second list unless they really believe what Psalm 127:3 communicates. I am sure you can identify many "gifts" from God in your life: your possessions, your abilities, your calling, your understanding of life's mysteries. These are all wonderful, but none of them carry your genetic code. Children do. The longer you live, the more you will grow to appreciate this mystery.

Appropriating the Promises

"The carrying out of God's promises is as certain as if already in the past tense." —JOHN BLANCHARD

The scripture highlighted in the last chapter establishes an important truth—your children are an inheritance from God and a reward from Him. So evidently, the Creator is very involved in your family. If you have dedicated your children to God, you can expect Him to overshadow them with His divine influence and care.

The collective mindset of the world seems to be descending deeper into darkness with each successive generation. Like a many-tentacled octopus, spiritual darkness is wrapping itself around the minds and hearts of our youth. Multiplied thousands are being strangled by drugs, alcohol, immorality, sexual perversion, gang violence, witchcraft, the occult, intellectualism, false religion and other diabolical plots and plans of the enemy. Thankfully, in the midst of all of this danger there is a place of protection—a place where our children can be preserved from harm. This refuge is made up of the 65 promises God has given concerning the offspring of those who are in a covenant relationship with Him.

Elizabeth and I pray these promises over our children often. We urge you to do the same. Go through these divine pledges one-by-one, commit them to memory and prayerfully speak them over your children whenever you can. Declaring these promises in faith releases them into manifestation. Remember, the Scripture teaches, "death and life are in the power of the tongue, and those who love it will eat its fruit" (Proverbs 18:21). Our words will either have a death-dealing or a life-imparting effect on our offspring.

You may want to use this book as a daily or nightly devotional, either by yourself or with your child. You could focus on a new promise in each sitting or stretch the experience out longer, studying one promise every week. After you finish, you should fully comprehend—and hopefully, apprehend—all of these divine pledges.

With each new promise, you will first encounter the key scripture, followed by the explanation that will help you appropriate the promise. Sometimes the same verse will contain several related promises. If so, that verse is simply repeated until each individual promise is showcased. After each explanation, you will find a suggested prayerful confession. You can repeat these prayers word-for-word, or be creative and pray as the Holy Spirit leads. Be sure to insert the name of your child in the blanks provided in the example prayers. You might want to actually write your child's name all through this book. If you have more than one child you should get a book for each child—and let each book be an individualized memorial your son or daughter will treasure for years to come.

However you do it, turn every page with a heart full of expectation and hope. This book could be much more than just a blessing; it could be the pivot on which the future of your family turns. May you look back after its completion and behold such a transformation that you will be heard exclaiming, "IT HAPPENED! THE WORD OF GOD REALLY WORKS!"

> *"God's promises are dependent and conditioned upon prayer to appropriate them and make them a conscious realization. The promises are inwrought in us, appropriated by us, and held in the arms of faith by prayer. Let it be noted that prayer gives the promises their efficiency, localizes and appropriates them, and utilizes them. Prayer puts the promises to practical and present uses."* —E.M. BOUNDS

Imparting the Promises

"That which God abundantly makes the subject of His promises, God's people should abundantly make the subject of their prayers." —JONATHAN EDWARDS

Not only is it important to pray these promises; you should find appropriate times when you can lay hands on your child as you confess these promises over his or her life. God will speak to your heart the perfect place and time. You can do it subtly, as if you are just expressing love with a touch. Or you can do it openly, especially if your child is fully receptive and cooperative.

"Laying on of hands" is listed as one of six foundational doctrines of the church in Hebrews 6:1-2. It is a Biblical practice, often used for purposes like healing and the ordination of elders. Interestingly, the first recorded instance of "laying on of hands" involved the blessing of children. In Genesis 48:16 we find Jacob laying hands on his grandsons, Ephraim and Manasseh, and praying, "The Angel who redeemed me from all evil, bless the lads...."

The "Angel" Jacob referred to was "the Angel of the LORD": something theologians call a Christophany—an appearance of the LORD Jesus Christ prior to His fleshly incarnation. Jacob wrestled with this "Angel" all night long, finally declaring, "I have seen God face to face." (Genesis 32:30, See Hosea 12:3-4.) This was the God of Abraham, Isaac and Jacob in a bodily form—the One who prospered Jacob and preserved him through all the seasons of his life. To this "Angel of the LORD" Jacob insisted, "I won't let you go until You bless me" (Genesis 32:26). God responded, the blessing was granted, and his name was changed to Israel—because he had power with God and with men.

Many years later Jacob was hoping to perpetuate this blessing by passing it on to his grandchildren. So he confessed this expectation over their lives with the laying on of hands. This was not a starchy ritual, performed with special ecclesiastical garments in a religious location. It was very real and down-to-earth—a private ceremony in a simple family gathering that resulted in a powerful impartation. Consequently, there was an invisible "blessing" that remained with those two grandsons the rest of their lives—manifesting in very visible and tangible ways. This event was so important, so pivotal, so multi-generational in its impact, that it landed Jacob among "the heroes of the faith" recorded in Hebrews 11. Isn't that an attention-grabber?

You need to also consider this—that Jacob did not have any written, Scriptural promises on which to base his faith. His primary motivation was the record of how God had perpetuated the "blessing" in his own family line: from his grandparents, Abraham and Sarah, to his parents, Isaac and Rebekah, then into his own life. Because his ancestors had walked in covenant with God, he expected to be blessed and to be a conduit of that blessing to his offspring. If Jacob, with his limited amount of information, could effectively pray over his grandchildren, how much more should we be able to seek God with high expectations! We have a much greater basis for our faith—the entire history of God's intervention on earth, in both the Old and New Testaments.

Jacob is not our only example in this area; Jesus prayerfully laid hands on children as well—and He is our chief role model. If the Son of God did it, we should. (See Matthew 19:13-15.) I can't help but wonder if the LORD confessed over those children some of the promises yet to be discussed in this book. If He did, the promises certainly had their impact. I wish we knew the "rest of the story": what those children became, and what great potential was awakened in their lives—just because Jesus laid His hands upon them and blessed them.

What about your children? What great potential and purpose can be released in their lives, just because you follow Jacob's example—and the LORD's example—praying over your offspring with the laying on of hands? You will never know until you try.

Waiting on the Promises

"Waiting for God is not laziness. Waiting for God is not going to sleep. Waiting for God is not the abandonment of effort." —G. CAMPBELL MORGAN

It would be so nice to be able to say that God's promises are always fulfilled immediately. Realistically, that's just not the case. Sometimes God *does* respond right away. But often we have to "earnestly contend for the faith" over a period of time (Jude 1:3 KJV). Those who propose to apprehend God's promises must be ready to "fight the good fight of faith"—daily warring against all the doubts and fears that so quickly cloud the mind and hinder us from "possessing our possessions." (1 Timothy 6:12, See Obadiah 17.) God gave the Land of Promise to the children of Israel, but still, they had to fight in order to obtain what was already rightfully theirs. And so it is with you and your seed.

Hebrews 11:33 reveals that "by faith" promises are obtained. Reading the whole chapter makes it clear that such an acquisition usually involves a process. Just look at some of the "Heroes of the Faith" mentioned:

- *Noah*—waited 120 years, and endured much rejection and ridicule, until his promise to come to pass.

- *Abraham and Sarah*—waited 25 years for their promise to come to pass, while they watched their aging bodies become increasingly less capable of fulfilling God's pledge.

- *Joseph*—waited 13 years for his promise to come to pass, while passing through a series of devastating betrayals and disappointments before being exalted by Pharaoh to a position of authority in Egypt.

No wonder the Scripture encourages us to be followers (or imitators) of "those who through faith and patience inherit the promises" (Hebrews 6:12). Patience is simply stick-to-itiveness, holding on to the promises until they manifest, enduring all the disheartening and frustrating setbacks that may come.

During this interim—between the promise and its fulfillment—we are simply called to *"wait on the LORD."* Probably the best definition of this spiritual discipline is this:

> *Abiding peacefully, prayerfully, patiently and per-severingly in His Presence, looking to the future with expectancy and hope.*

Waiting on God is persistence in prayer, yet simultaneously, it is a willingness to accept God's timing on the matter. Those who embrace this heart-attitude maintain an underlying trust that the Father will ultimately watch over His Word to perform it—when it is most advantageous and most effective to do so. There are key passages in the Bible that share the wisdom, the value and the necessity of *"waiting on God."* Here are some of the best:

> *Wait on the LORD; be of good courage, and He shall strengthen your heart; wait, I say, on the LORD!*
> (Psalms 27:14)

> *Rest in the LORD, and wait patiently for Him...*
> (Psalms 37:7)

> *I wait for the LORD, my soul waits, and in His Word I do hope. My soul waits for the LORD, more than those who watch for the morning—Yes, more than those who watch for the morning.* (Psalms 130:5-6)

> *But those who wait on the LORD shall renew their strength; they shall mount up with wings like eagles, they shall run and not be weary, they shall walk and not faint.* (Isaiah 40:31)

So go ahead. Spread your "eagle wings" and soar. See things from a higher perspective. Don't exhaust yourself, batting the air like a sparrow; glide like an eagle. Let the wind of the Spirit carry you.

Most importantly, if at all possible, make a quality decision to love and enjoy your child at the "place" he or she is at—while you are "waiting" for God to take that son or daughter to the place he or she needs to be. As you pass through this intermediate phase, you may want to implement the wisdom Diane Loomans shares in her wonderful poem, reminiscing on her role as a parent:

If I had my child to raise over again.
I'd build self-esteem first and the house later.
I'd finger paint more and point the finger less.
I would do less correcting and more connecting.
I'd take my eyes off my watch and watch with my eyes.
I would care to know less and know to care more.
I'd take more hikes and fly more kites.
I'd stop playing serious and seriously play.
I would run through more fields and gaze at more stars.
I'd do more hugging and less tugging.
I'd see the oak tree in the acorn more often.
I would be firm less often and affirm much more.
I'd model less about the love of power.
And more about the power of love.

Yes, I agree. We need to see the "the oak tree in the acorn"— and celebrate the expected outcome daily in prayer, as we wait for our "acorns" to germinate and grow. Of all things, we need to concentrate on modeling "the power of love." And we need to let the promise resound within our minds often:

Blessed are all those who wait for Him. (Isaiah 30:18)

The Lord is Building Your House

"There are two ways to live your life. One is as though nothing is a miracle. The other is as though everything is a miracle." —ALBERT EINSTEIN

So there it is! The foundation has been laid. Now you're ready to build—but remember to always acknowledge God's role in the process. The first verse of Psalm 127 (a chapter mentioned often in this book) says it so well—"Except the LORD build the house, they labor in vain who build it." So invite God now to be the Manager of your "Family Construction Project." He will gladly comply, for He has already declared:

> *The curse of the LORD is on the house of the wicked, but*
> *HE BLESSES THE HOME OF THE JUST.*
>
> (Proverbs 3:33)

God is very definite in the proclamation of this promise, so you should be just as definite in echoing it. Boldly approach God's throne with a Jacob-like attitude in prayer, crying out, "I will not let You go, LORD, until You do this—until You bless my home—and until You bless my offspring. You are the God of Abraham, Isaac and Jacob. You have plans that stretch from generation to generation. I believe that Your best belongs to my seed. I claim a great breakthrough—in Jesus' Name." (See Matthew 22:32.)

When this breakthrough comes, be sure to contact us, by mail or email, and share your praise report. We love you and we're praying that God will truly bring forth—

A MIRACLE FOR YOUR FAMILY!

PART TWO

The Promises

...*He has given to us exceedingly great and precious*
PROMISES.

(2 Peter 1:4 MKJV)

PROMISE:

1. A declaration that one will do or refrain from doing something specified

2. A legally binding declaration that gives the person to whom it is made a right to expect or to claim the performance or forbearance of a specified act.

1 *Life*

"I call heaven and earth as witnesses today against you, that I have set before you life and death, blessing and cursing; therefore choose life, that both you and your descendants may live;

That you may love the LORD your God, that you may obey His voice, and that you may cling to Him, for He is your life and the length of your days; and that you may dwell in the land which the LORD swore to your fathers, to Abraham, Isaac, and Jacob, to give them." (Deuteronomy 30:19-20)

First, this promise can mean a long and prosperous physical life. (See Psalms 91:14-16.) More importantly, it means "life" in a mental, emotional and spiritual sense. Anger, pride, lust, depression, fear, rebellion—these attitudes have a death-dealing effect on parents and their impressionable children. A home dominated by these attitudes is very dark and full of "death" indeed!

When parents "choose life," they tend to walk in attitudes that are the polar opposite: love, humility, selflessness, joy, faith and obedience to God. These life-giving attitudes of heart are then passed on to their children—so that they are also embraced by the life of God.

PRAYER/CONFESSION

LORD, I claim this promise from Deuteronomy 30. Because I choose to live for truth and to live for God, I believe spiritual "life" will be passed to my child. I pray that he/she will continue the family tradition of "choosing life" and be filled with the very life of God. In doing so, _____ will escape the death-dealing results of a life of sin. I confess that the life-giving attributes of God's nature will fill our home, our lives and our relationship: love, joy, peace, righteousness and goodness. Yes, I "choose life," for myself and for my offspring—in Jesus' Name, Amen (Let it be so)!

2 *Obeying God*

"I call heaven and earth as witnesses today against you, that I have set before you life and death, blessing and cursing; therefore choose life, that both you and your descendants may live;

That you may love the LORD your God, that you may obey His voice, and that you may cling to Him, for He is your life and the length of your days; and that you may dwell in the land which the LORD swore to your fathers, to Abraham, Isaac, and Jacob, to give them." (Deuteronomy 30:19-20)

When we, as believers, "choose life," automatically that involves "choosing obedience." On the other hand, if we disobey God, we are "choosing death." Simple to understand. No mincing words on this issue. God warned Adam and Eve in the beginning, "You may freely eat of every tree in the garden, but you shall not eat of the tree of knowledge of good and evil. For in the day that you eat of it you shall surely die" (Genesis 2:16-17).

When they chose disobedience, they chose death—and passed the curse of death on to their offspring. Those who "choose life" walk in obedience to God. In doing so, they pass the legacy of life and obedience on to their seed. You've heard the old saying, "Like father, like son." That's the way it works.

PRAYER/CONFESSION

LORD, I claim this promise from Deuteronomy 30. I refuse the spiritual "death" that results from a life of sin; instead, I "choose life." I choose righteousness. I choose to walk in obedience to Your Word and Your will. In response, I believe You will cause a "spirit of obedience" to rest upon _____ . Instead of the curse of death, he/she will inherit a legacy of life—physically, mentally, emotionally and spiritually—and obediently walk in it all the days of his/her life—in Jesus' Name, Amen (Let it be so)!

3 Circumcision of the Heart

"And the LORD your God will circumcise your heart and the heart of your descendants, to love the LORD your God with all your heart and with all your soul, that you may live."
(Deuteronomy 30:6)

Circumcision is the surgical removal of the male foreskin, usually performed shortly after birth. It is a symbol of God "cutting away" from our hearts the "covering" of fleshly attitudes that prevent us from loving and serving God.

Often we trust in mere instruction and discipline to effect this change in our children. God is promising to do it supernaturally. Convincing a child through logic and reason is nowhere near as powerful as an encounter with God that transforms that child from within. Praise God! The Most High pledges to do that very thing. (See Romans 2:28-29.)

PRAYER/CONFESSION

LORD, I claim for my child a circumcised heart, that you will "cut away" the worldliness, the carnality and the sensuality that could otherwise corrupt him/her. I acknowledge that this is a promised divine deliverance, a supernatural act of God, and not something I can force by mere religious instruction. I trust You, LORD, to work this awesome, internal transformation in _____ : a circumcised heart—in Jesus' Name, Amen (Let it be so)!

4 *Love for God*

"And the LORD your God will circumcise your heart and the heart of your descendants, to love the LORD your God with all your heart and with all your soul, that you may live."
(Deuteronomy 30:6)

Once a person's heart is circumcised, the potential is awakened of passionately loving the heavenly Father. The Scripture explains "the love of God is shed abroad in our hearts" by the Holy Spirit (Romans 5:5). So this is evidently a work of God.

God promises that those He "circumcises" will love God with ALL their hearts. When this truly happens, children will automatically be attracted to those things God loves—the things that have eternal value. This impartation of love is so important that Jesus even climaxed His ministry by praying that the Father's love would indwell all New Covenant believers. (See John 17:26.) If He prayed this over us, we should certainly pray it over our children.

PRAYER/CONFESSION

LORD, I admit that only You can awaken love for the things of God in my child's heart. I trust You to do that. I believe _____ will not only love You, but love the things that You love; like truth, righteousness and kindness. I believe that _____ will be a very loving child: loving family, loving others in the body of Christ, and loving the lost of this world who have not yet found their way. Yes, I confess—the love of God will be shed abroad in the heart of my child—in Jesus' Name, Amen (Let it be so)!

5 *Covenant Relationship*

> *"Therefore know that the LORD your God, He is God, the faithful God who keeps covenant and mercy for a thousand generations with those who love Him and keep His commandments."* (Deuteronomy 7:9)

A covenant is an agreement between two or more parties, each binding himself to fulfill certain obligations. When we surrender our hearts to the LORD Jesus Christ, we enter a covenant relationship with Him. He in turn obligates Himself to always be with us, forgive us of our sins, fulfill His promises and preserve us unto eternal life.

This covenantal arrangement overflows to our offspring also. Of course, they must surrender to God in order to receive the fullness of all the covenantal blessings and benefits, but this verse implies that they are automatically on a certain level of covenant connection with God—simply because of parents who are already walking with God. Want proof? Remember what God said to Noah, "Behold, I establish My covenant with you and *with your descendents after you*" (Genesis 9:9, emphasis by author). The God of Noah is our God. The way He felt then is surely the way He feels now.

PRAYER/CONFESSION

LORD, I confess that I am in a covenant relationship with You and I believe my descendents are as well. I am committed to You and You are committed to me. I believe You will honor our relationship by committing Yourself also to the welfare of my son/daughter… in body, soul and spirit. I believe You will grant _____ grace to walk in a covenant relationship with You and prosper all the days of his/her life—in Jesus' Name, Amen (Let it be so)!

6 *Mercy*

"Therefore know that the LORD your God, He is God, the faithful God who keeps covenant and mercy for a thousand generations with those who love Him and keep His commandments." (Deuteronomy 7:9)

Mercy is compassion shown especially to those of criminal behavior. In a sense, we have all been criminals, for we have all committed the crime of breaking God's laws. Titus 3:5 reveals that God saves us, not because of "works of righteousness," but because of "His mercy." According to the key verse above, God stores up a reservoir of mercy for our seed also—so when they need it, His divine compassion will overflow their lives.

God promised David He would preserve his dynasty forever. If his offspring sinned, they would be chastened, but divine mercy would protect the Davidic throne. When Solomon, David's son, petitioned God to bless the temple at its dedication, he reminded the LORD of this promise—that "sure mercies" would hover over the seed of David (Isaiah 55:3). God responded by sending such intense glory in the temple, the priests could not even enter (2 Chronicles 6:41-7:3). This event illustrates how powerfully God honors foreparents who serve Him. If He did it then for David's seed, He will do it again for ours—and God's mercy and glory will overflow their lives.

PRAYER/CONFESSION

LORD, I believe You are the faithful God who stores up mercy for the offspring of the righteous. If my child errs in life, I believe Your mercy will guide him/her back to You, to find forgiveness, cleansing and restoration. LORD have mercy upon _____ and deliver him/her in every trial, temptation, failure or disappointment. I appeal to You, O Father of mercies, to make my son/daughter a vessel of mercy, on whom You will pour out Your glory and through whom You will express Your mercy to others—in Jesus' Name, Amen (Let it be so)!

7 Salvation

"Believe on the LORD Jesus Christ, and you will be saved,
you and your household."   (Acts 16:31)

Amazingly, this promise was not made to a seasoned saint, but to an unsaved man on the verge of suicide. God had just responded to the praise of Paul and Silas by sending an earthquake that shook the prison doors open. The Philippian jailer—assuming the prisoners had escaped—was about to kill himself. Paul cried, "Do yourself no harm, for we are all here." The jailer responded, "What must I do to be saved?" Paul replied, "Believe on the LORD Jesus Christ, and you will be saved, you and your household" (Acts 16:25-31).

If a deeply troubled man, just being introduced to the faith, could receive this divine commitment, how much more those who have fought the good fight of faith for years! Yes, we who believe have a legal right to claim our families for the Kingdom, for the King has pledged, "I will contend with him who contends with you, and *I will save your children*" (Isaiah 49:25). Salvation means *deliverance*, so God is promising to *deliver* our children—from every evil thing that could possibly ensnare their souls.

PRAYER/CONFESSION

LORD, on the basis of these promises, I claim salvation for my son/daughter. I believe You will contend with any satanic force that may be contending with our family. You are the LORD of hosts, the God of an army of angels. These heavenly beings have been "sent forth to minister for...the heirs of salvation." So dispatch them, LORD, to protect and defend my child. I pray You will save _____ from the enticement of sin and the deception of this world; and grant him/her all the benefits of salvation: forgiveness, grace, wholeness and the gift of eternal life—in Jesus' Name, Amen (Let it be so)! (Hebrews 1:14)

8 The Legacy of Integrity

The righteous man walks in his integrity; his children are blessed after him. (Proverbs 20:7)

The word "integrity" means firm adherence to a code of moral values. Men and women of integrity have a passion for honesty, sincerity and truth. Such traits tend to produce success and prosperity, and normally result in a life well lived.

There are two primary reasons why descendents of such persons are "blessed." First, adherence to such a value system creates stability in the home: a healthy atmosphere conducive to raising healthy children. Second, the legacy of a lifestyle of integrity with all of its benefits is passed down to generations following.

Two other versions express this same passage in pleasant terms. The Contemporary English Version explains, "Good people live right, and God blesses the children who follow their example." The Living Bible concludes, "It is a wonderful heritage to have an honest father."

PRAYER/CONFESSION

FATHER GOD, I thank You first for the grace to walk in integrity that I may pass this heritage on to my child. When deceit is more convenient, let me be honest instead. When compromise entices, let commitment surge within me. When hypocrisy stalks me, let sincerity guard my soul. When immorality woos my mind, let my heart remain pure and my standards, strong. Help me to be a role model for my child. Grace me to be strong in these areas of character, then transfer this legacy of inner strength to _____ with all of its benefits and blessings—in Jesus' Name, Amen (Let it be so)!

9 *Provision*

I have been young, and now am old; yet have I not seen
the righteous forsaken, nor his descendants begging bread.
(Psalms 37:25)

What a comfort to know this—that if we, as parents, walk in righteousness, God will see to it that our offspring have an ample supply of necessary natural provisions! Certainly we can find exceptions to this in a world full of poverty and destitution. However, generally speaking, we can expect this to be the case.

There are extreme examples in Scripture that should build our faith. What about God giving Joseph such divine insight that the needs of his family were met during seven years of famine? What about the manna that came down from heaven during Israel's wilderness journey? What about the widow woman and her son, on the verge of starvation—then Elijah prophesied that a meal barrel and a cruse of oil would never fail to produce? Of course, there is no more powerful example than Jesus multiplying the loaves and fishes and feeding the multitudes! If He took care of His people then—He can certainly take care of us and our children now.

PRAYER/CONFESSION

O GOD, I confess over my family that You are the LORD OUR PROVIDER. I believe You will always supply ample provision for my child. Even during hard times, times of recession or depression, I pray that _____ needs will always be met, that he/she will always have sufficient food and shelter. Moreover, I praise You for leading _____ into the right career choice, and giving him/ her the best job opportunities, the best promotions and the highest wages possible. I declare before Your throne that my seed will never have to beg. Favor will go before _____ and golden doors of opportunity will continually open before him/her, both naturally and spiritually—in Jesus' Name, Amen (Let it be so)!

10 Inheriting the Land

Who is the man who fears the LORD? He will instruct
him in the way he should choose.
His soul will abide in prosperity, and his descendants
will inherit the land.   (Psalms 25:12-13 NASU)

This promise evidently means more than just acquiring real
estate. On a higher level, "inheriting the land" speaks of having
prominence and influence in order to transform individuals or
society as a whole with the values and character of God's Kingdom.
This can happen for the offspring of believers on a local level or
worldwide, "inheriting" everything from neighborhoods to nations.
(See Isaiah 54:3, Psalms 2:8.)

A good example is Martin Luther King, Jr. Not only were his
parents strong Christians, his father was a preacher. Around the
age of 17, the "ministry mantle" passed to Martin. Though he never
held a political office or owned large masses of real estate, Martin
Luther King, Jr. "inherited the land" in a more profound way. As
he selflessly began promoting racial equality in his native Alabama,
God began promoting him to a place of international prominence.
If you have surrendered your life to the LORD Jesus Christ, expect
him to awaken in your son or daughter a similar potential of being
a world-changer and a history-maker.

PRAYER/CONFESSION

LORD, I pray that _____ will "inherit the land," that
he/she will be a person of influence in this world. I believe that
through my son/daughter, You will mold and shape the values of
his/her generation in a positive and powerful way. I also confess that
_____ will inherit the land in a literal sense, ruling and
reigning with You in the Kingdom of God to come, forever
and ever—in Jesus' Name, Amen (Let it be so)!

11 *The Outpouring of God's Spirit*

*"For I will pour water on him who is thirsty, and floods
on the dry ground; I will pour My Spirit on your descendants,
and My blessing on your offspring."* (Isaiah 44:3)

The most important thing that any child can have is a real, personal encounter with the living God. It is not enough for children to merely witness the reality of God in the lives of their parents; they must experience it for themselves. If we thirst after God, the Father promises to do that—pouring out the living water of His Spirit upon their lives.

God has promised that He will be *"with the generation of the righteous"* (Psalms 14:5, emphasis by author). Therefore, if we "thirst after righteousness" and walk in the "paths of righteousness," God promises to be with our offspring—influencing their lives with His outpoured Presence (Matthew 5:6, Proverbs 2:20). Certainly, a child must make a personal decision claiming Jesus as LORD in order for the Savior to actually dwell in their hearts, but until that spiritual rebirth takes place, our decision to serve God will apparently cause His Spirit to be with them in a special way, drawing them unto Himself.

PRAYER/CONFESSION

LORD, I thirst for You. I pray that Your living water will fill my soul, and flow through my child as well. I confess that my son/daughter will never be like a desert, but will blossom with the beauty of the LORD and fruit for Your Kingdom. Because I thirst for righteousness, I trust that Your Presence will be with my child always: guarding, guiding and instructing him/her in every situation. As _____ begins seeking You and drinking of Your Presence, I pray that this spiritual water will become in him/her a well of water springing up into everlasting life—in Jesus' Name, Amen (Let it be so)!

12 The Outpouring of God's Blessing

"For I will pour water on him who is thirsty, and floods on the dry ground; I will pour My Spirit on your descendants, and My blessing on your offspring.
They will spring up among the grass like willows by the watercourses." (Isaiah 44:3-4)

In this passage, God promises to pour out two things on the children of those who thirst after Him: His Spirit and His blessing. A blessing is any benefit from God that causes happiness, fulfillment or wholeness in a person's life. When God pours out His blessing on our children, we can expect their needs to be met: physically, materially, mentally, emotionally and spiritually.

Blessed children are happy children. They do not have fragmented personalities and are not empty-hearted. They are fulfilled and contented, walking in God's purpose. They tend to then pass the blessing on to others that the blessing of God might fill the earth.

PRAYER/CONFESSION

LORD GOD, I thank You by faith for Your blessing descending on my child. Let it pour down like the rain of heaven. I believe that this divine blessing will be evidenced in every area of my child's life: physically, materially, socially, emotionally, mentally and spiritually. Your Word declares that "the blessing of the LORD makes one rich and He adds no sorrow with it." Thank You for enriching _____ with all the benefits that You have promised in Your Word—crowning his/her life with the best that heaven can provide—in Jesus' Name, Amen (Let it be so)! (Proverbs 10:22)

13 Spiritual Growth

"For I will pour water on him who is thirsty, and floods on the dry ground; I will pour My Spirit on your descendants, and My blessing on your offspring.

They will spring up among the grass like willows by the watercourses." (Isaiah 44:3-4)

When parents walk in truth, their relationship with God provides a "stream of living waters" constantly flowing through the lives of their children. This brings nurture and growth to them spiritually. Children are constantly "watered" by the example of their parents and the training they receive—and should constantly grow in God as a result. In fact, living trees never stop growing. The Scripture describes John the Baptist and even the LORD Jesus, when they were children—"growing" and becoming "strong in spirit" (Luke 1:80, 2:40).

God's people should expect the same for their children. As our key verse terms it, their offspring will "spring up…like willows by the watercourses." Willow trees, because of their drooping branches, speak especially of humility before God—bowing before Him submissively and adoringly all our days. In this passage, our seed are characterized this way. What a beautiful analogy!

PRAYER/CONFESSION

LORD, I believe that _____ will spring up before You and be humble, submissive and adoring toward You all his/her days. I confess that because You promised to pour out Your Spirit and Your blessing on my offspring, it will come to pass. _____ will not be stunted spiritually, but will ever grow in the things of God, nourished by the constant flow of the river of God's presence in his/her life—in Jesus' Name, Amen (Let it be so)!

14 *Divine Instruction*

*"All your children shall be taught by the LORD, and great
shall be the peace of your children."* (Isaiah 54:13)

This verse is literally talking about the offspring of New
Jerusalem, the eternal city of God. Yet God identifies New Jerusalem
as "the bride, the Lamb's wife" (Revelation 21:9). So on a prophetic
and symbolic level, a promise to the children of New Jerusalem is
a promise to the children of those who make up "the bride" that
this city represents.

How comforting it is to know that God Himself will instruct
our children! We can only go so far in helping them to understand
the mysteries of the Kingdom of God. We can fill their minds with
information, but only God can fill their hearts with revelation—
which He promises to do in this passage. He will grant them insight
into human character and teach them how to be successful in every
area of life.

PRAYER/CONFESSION

*LORD, I believe that no one can come to You unless the Holy Spirit
draws him. I also believe that when this happens, Your Spirit intends
to lead that person—step-by-step—into ALL truth. I claim this kind
of divine instruction for my son/daughter. I confess that the "Spirit
of wisdom" will open _____ eyes to the truth and reveal to
him/her the "deep things of God." I also believe You will train
_____ how to have fruitful and godly relationships and a
successful life in every way—in Jesus' Name, Amen (Let it be so)!
(Ephesians 1:17, 1 Corinthians 2:10)*

15 *Great Peace*

"All your children shall be taught by the LORD, and great shall be the peace of your children." (Isaiah 54:13)

Peace is calmness of mind and heart. It may not mean a life free from stress, but it certainly means maintaining a tranquil attitude—resting in the LORD—even in midst of traumatic circumstances. Jesus is called "the Prince of peace" (Isaiah 9:6). When He's invited to reign in a person's heart, He brings many gifts, including peace. He promised His followers, "My peace I give to you...Let not your heart be troubled." (John 14:27 MKJV).

In our key passage, God promises an overflow of His peace into the lives of our offspring. This means much more than just human emotion. The Bible describes it as "peace in the Holy Spirit" and "the peace of God which passes all understanding" (Romans 14:17, Philippians 4:7 MKJV). No wonder Isaiah 54:13 calls it "great peace." In a strife-filled world, how needed is this pledge from the lips of the Almighty!

PRAYER/CONFESSION:

LORD, I believe, as Your Word promises, that You will extend peace to me "like a river," and that this peace will flow over the soul of my son/ daughter as well. I pray that _____ will be preserved from the mentally and emotionally damaging things that can create stress, strife and anxiety in our hearts. May _____ always maintain "peace WITH God" (a harmonious relationship with You) and may the "peace OF God" always abide within him/her. Your Word declares that You are the "God of peace." I pray that _____ will so completely yield to Your peaceful nature that he/she even becomes a means of passing this wonderful gift on to others—fulfilling the call to be a "peacemaker" in the earth—in Jesus' Name, Amen (Let it be so)! (Isaiah 66:12, Romans 5:1; 16:20, Philippians 4:7, Matthew 5:9)

16 Imparted Righteousness

But the mercy of the LORD is from everlasting to everlasting on those who fear Him, and His righteousness to children's children.   (Psalms 103:17)

This verse promises, not humanly attained righteousness, but God's righteousness passed to the offspring of those who fear the LORD. This wonderful "gift of righteousness" also comes in response to faith (Romans 5:17). "Abraham believed God, and it was accounted to him for righteousness." (Galatians 3:6, See Romans 4:19-25.) Certainly, Abraham's offspring did not automatically inherit this imparted righteousness from God just by virtue of their natural birth, but they did inherit *the knowledge* of how to access this wonderful opportunity. And so it is with us.

While the adherents of most world religions strive to reach the elusive goal of righteousness through works, Christian parents can teach their offspring to set their faith on the cross where Jesus was made to be "sin for us, that we might become the righteousness of God in Him." (2 Corinthians 5:21, See Romans 10:9-10.)

PRAYER/CONFESSION

LORD GOD, I pray first that my child will understand the righteousness that comes as a gift from God. I also pray and believe that he/she will access this righteousness by faith and respond by living righteously before You all of his/her days. May _____ "hunger and thirst for righteousness," and as a result, be "filled with the fruits of righteousness"—in Jesus' Name, Amen (Let it be so)! (Matthew 5:6, Philippians 1:11)

17 Hope for Restoration

"There is hope in your future," says the LORD, "that your children shall come back to their own border."

(Jeremiah 31:17)

This was initially a reference to the children of Israel who were captives of war, carried away into the bondage of Babylon. Enslaved in a foreign nation, they longed to be free and to see their children return one day to the Promised Land. God testified in this passage that their hopes would be fulfilled.

This scripture can also be claimed in a spiritual sense concerning backslidden children of godly parents. Though their offspring have been "carried away" into the "bondage" of a worldly lifestyle and "enslavement" to sin, committed parents can trust that their offspring will be brought back to the "border" of a spiritual Land of Promise: a place of blessed and fruitful relationship with the Most High God.

On a higher level, this promise is applicable to all of us, celebrating the hope we have of returning to the perfection of the original paradise state, returning to the "border" of the Garden of Eden and the intimacy with God that our foreparents knew.

PRAYER/CONFESSION

LORD, I confess that as long as there is a God in heaven, there is hope. If _____ ever strays in any way from Your will and purpose, or if this has already happened, I confess that my child will always come back to the "boundary" of the truth. I claim that _____ will be blessed to dwell in a spiritual "Land of Promise," a land filled with both Your written Word promises and any, living Word promises You have spoken over his/her life. Most importantly, I confess that _____ will ultimately be restored to the perfection of paradise, when You return in glory—in Jesus' Name, Amen (Let it be so)!

18   Olive Plants

Your wife shall be like a fruitful vine in the very heart of your house, your children like olive plants all around your table. (Psalms 128:3)

There are three primary aspects to this wonderful promise:

(1) *Fruitbearers*—The main emphasis is that olive trees bear fruit. Symbolically, this means that the children of God's people will be fruitbearers. They will bear the fruit of the Spirit (the character of God), the fruit of good works and the fruit of souls won into the Kingdom of God. (See Galatians 5:22-23, Ephesians 5:9, Philippians 4:17, John 4:36.)

(2) *Spiritually hardy*—Olive trees are also very hardy plants that can grow well in rough and rocky terrain. So the children of the righteous should be very capable—through the grace of God—to handle the rough, rocky territory they face in life.

(3) *Anointed*—Olive oil is a strong, Biblical symbol for the anointing of the Holy Spirit. The anointing is even referred to as "the oil of gladness" and "the oil of joy" (Psalms 45:7, Hebrews 1:9, Isaiah 61:3). So God is promising that the children of the righteous will be producers of the anointing—that they will manifest the power of God as they minister the truth to others.

PRAYER/CONFESSION

LORD GOD, on the basis of Psalm 128:3, I pray my child will be like an olive plant at my table, that _____ will bear much fruit and be a blessing to others and a praise to God in the earth. If he/she faces rough and rocky places in life, I believe my child will be able to endure with the help of God. I confess that the "oil of gladness" (the anointing of the Holy Spirit) will flow through _____ powerfully to extend the Kingdom of God in this world. I speak these things knowing that Your Word will not return void. It will accomplish what You have declared—in Jesus' Name, Amen (Let it be so)!

19 Holy unto the Lord

For the unbelieving husband is sanctified by the wife,
and the unbelieving wife is sanctified by the husband; otherwise
your children would be unclean, but now they are holy.

(1 Corinthians 7:14)

This is a comforting promise, especially in divided homes where only one parent is serving God. First, the unbelieving spouse is "sanctified" (set apart for God) by the commitment of the believing partner. This does not mean that person's sins are forgiven even when no repentance is present. It simply means that person is consecrated to God by the prayerfulness and faith of the saved spouse. It seems that God is "legally" released to deal more profoundly with that person as a result.

In like manner, the children of this union are also, automatically, considered "holy unto the LORD" (separated from the world and dedicated to the Father). To receive the full benefits of salvation, God will certainly require children to personally consecrate themselves to God, but still, the path has been cleared for them— and the way has been made much easier.

PRAYER/CONFESSION

LORD GOD, I declare that my son/daughter is "holy unto the LORD,"
dedicated to You and consecrated to Your purposes. I believe You will
honor my commitment to You by separating _____ from
the world and drawing him/her to Yourself. I pray and believe that
_____ will be kept from the defilement and corruption
that is so rampant in the earth today. Instead, I confess that by
grace, my son/daughter will have a passion for holiness
and be pleasing in Your sight—in Jesus' Name,
Amen (Let it be so)!

20 Proclaimers of God's Word

"As for Me," says the LORD, "this is My covenant with them: My Spirit who is upon you, and My words which I have put in your mouth, shall not depart from your mouth, nor from the mouth of your descendants, nor from the mouth of your descendants' descendants," says the LORD, "from this time and forevermore." (Isaiah 59:21)

Vision is generational. God authors a certain revelation of His Word in a man or woman of faith—then, in order for it to reach maximum effectiveness and full fruition, the same truth is often passed to that person's offspring.

John and Charles Wesley shook the world in their day with the revelation of the true Gospel. However, it did not originate with them. They inherited their insights and passion for God from Samuel and Susanna Wesley, God-loving parents who planted the seed of truth within their hearts. Wouldn't it be wonderful if your child ended up as fruitful in the work of God as these two giants of the faith? If it happened in the Wesley home, it can happen in yours.

PRAYER/CONFESSION

LORD GOD, I thank You for all the truths You have revealed to me. I declare that these truths will not end with me. Part of the legacy I pass to my son/daughter are the God-given insights that have transformed my life. LORD, You prayed for Your disciples, saying, "Father...I have given them the words which You have given Me." I pray the same for _____ , that he/she will receive the same revelation of truth You have given me. I pray that my child will be personally transformed by this insight, that he/she will always live according to the truth, and that _____ will be a powerful voice of truth in a world full of spiritual deception—in Jesus' Name, Amen (Let it be so)! (John 17:8)

21 *Angelic Protection*

*"Take heed that you do not despise one of these little ones,
for I say to you that in heaven their angels always see the face
of My Father who is in heaven."* (Matthew 18:10)

When Jesus made this statement, evidently, He was referring to
ALL children—not just the children of believers. First, He warned
against any cruel treatment of "little ones." Second, He revealed
that one or more angels are assigned to each child; and that these
heavenly beings consult with the Father concerning any adverse
situations in that child's life. Apparently, these "guardian angels"
are ever ready to request divine intervention or retribution. If this is
true for ALL children, how much MORE the children of God's people!
(See Daniel 12:1-2.)

Hebrews 1:7 explains that angels are "ministering spirits" sent
forth to minister for the heirs of salvation. That means they work
behind the scenes of your life to bring forth God's best in everything
that pertains to you—most importantly, your children. Jesus confided
that if He asked, the Father would have sent twelve legions of angels
to defend Him from danger. Certainly He can do the same for any
child committed to His care.

PRAYER/CONFESSION

*LORD GOD, You are the LORD of hosts, the God of an army of angels
who are poised and ready for battle. I confess that at least one angel
is assigned to constantly watch over _____ , to insure divine
protection and provision in his/her life. According to Your Word,
many centuries ago, just one angel brought total defeat to the entire
Assyrian army. So one angel in my child's life is sufficient to bring
deliverance in every area of need. Yet I believe that there are many
ministering spirits actively engaged in ministering to our family—
that we might inherit ALL the benefits of salvation. I praise You that
this very thing is taking place right now—in Jesus' Name,
Amen (Let it be so)! (See 2 Kings 19:35.)*

22 *Clinging to God*

"I call heaven and earth as witnesses today against you, that I have set before you life and death, blessing and cursing; therefore choose life, that both you and your descendants may live;

That you may love the LORD your God, that you may obey His voice, and that you may cling to Him, for He is your life and the length of your days; and that you may dwell in the land which the LORD swore to your fathers, to Abraham, Isaac, and Jacob, to give them."   (Deuteronomy 30:19-20)

Have you ever seen a scared or troubled child "clinging" to Mommy's skirt or Daddy's pants with all his or her might? This is the picture I get when I read this promise. As parents grow in their relationship with God, more and more, they assume the posture of "clinging" to the Creator in times of trouble and in the midst of a very wicked world. This impresses the minds of children, often compelling them to maintain the same stance. People of this world tend to cling to a rope that unravels—and they often perish as a result: mentally, emotionally and even physically. God's offspring cling to an unbreakable chain of hope in God's promises. At the end is the "anchor of the soul," going beyond the veil of time.

PRAYER/CONFESSION

LORD GOD, I first confess that not only do I believe in You, I also "cling" to You. In times of difficulty, my intentions are to hold on to You with all of my might. I pray You will awaken this depth of dependency in my son/daughter. Instead of "clinging" to the things of the world for fulfillment and satisfaction, may _____ always "cling" to You—with a tenacity that will never let go. I confess that this kind of spiritual stick-to-itiveness will be the prevailing attitude of my child's heart all the days of his/her life— in Jesus' Name, Amen (Let it be so)!

23 Created for God's Glory

*"Fear not, for I am with you; I will bring your
descendants from the east, and gather you from the west;*
*I will say to the north, 'Give them up!' and to the south,
'Do not keep them back!' Bring My sons from afar, and My
daughters from the ends of the earth—*
*Everyone who is called by My name, whom I have created
for My glory; I have formed him, yes, I have made him."*
(Isaiah 43:5-7)

When we read these verses, we should lift our eyes toward
God in worshipful awe. God actually refers to our offspring as *His*
sons and *His* daughters. In other words, God is saying, "Because
they belong to you, they belong to Me. Because you have named
My Name over their lives, I claim them as My own."

God also asserts that our offspring have been created for His
glory. The world system would like to seduce our seed to spend
their lives giving "glory" to that which has little or no value. Declare
over your child that his talents or her abilities will never be wasted
in vain pursuits, but that their lives will be invested only in that
which gives praise, honor and acclaim to the Creator.

PRAYER/CONFESSION

*LORD GOD, I pray first that You will gather _____ unto
Yourself and deliver him/her from all the enticements and entrapments
of this world. Because of the covenant we share, all that I have
belongs to You. So I confess Your Name over _____ and I
believe You will claim him/her as Your own. I trust You to prevent
_____ from devoting his/her life to that which would give
glory to human achievement alone. Instead, awaken such
divinely inspired purpose in my child that glory ascends to You
from his/her life—in Jesus' Name, Amen (Let it be so)!*

24 An Enduring House

"Then it shall be, if you heed all that I command you, walk in My ways, and do what is right in My sight, to keep My statutes and My commandments, as My servant David did, then I will be with you and build for you an enduring house, as I built for David, and will give Israel to you."

(1 Kings 11:38)

Although this particular promise was originally spoken to an individual (Jeroboam, the son of Nebat), it is applicable to any parents who strive to keep God's commandments. First, God is saying that the family line will "endure"—it will continue from generation to generation.

Second, God is pledging to the righteous, "Your children will have a spirit of endurance. They will fight the good fight of faith. They will be tenacious in the face of rejection or opposition. They will persevere in living the truth, when others are weak and succumb to the influence of an evil world." Enduring families and enduring children: that's what this two-fold promise is all about!

PRAYER/CONFESSION

LORD GOD, my passion is to heed Your commandments and walk in Your ways. Therefore, I have a right to expect the fulfillment of this promise. In an age of great instability in many families, I believe that I will have "an enduring house." I pray that a spirit of endurance will also rest upon my son/daughter, that _____ will always be able to "endure temptation" and "endure hardship as a good soldier of Jesus Christ." I confess by faith that _____ will be able to "run with endurance" the race set before him/her and successfully make it all the way to heaven—in Jesus' Name, Amen (Let it be so)!
(James 1:12, 2 Timothy 2:3, Hebrews 12:1)

25 *Increase*

*The L*ORD *shall increase you more and more, you and your children.* (Psalms 115:14 KJV)

In this verse, God promises "increase," but doesn't specify the particular areas. Most likely, this divine pledge should be realized in every arena of our lives, and the lives of our children—ever-increasing peace and joy, ever-increasing wisdom and knowledge, ever-increasing effectiveness and fruitfulness, ever-increasing intimacy with God and sensitivity to His will, and even ever-increasing material prosperity.

In referencing certain churches under his care, Paul explained, "I planted, Apollos watered, but God gave *the increase*" (1 Corinthians 3:6). In like manner, parents are called to plant seeds of truth in the lives of their children, then water the seed with much love, but God is the One who brings forth *increase*—from "faith to faith," from "strength to strength," and from "glory to glory" (Romans 1:17, Psalms 84:7, 2 Corinthians 3:18)!

PRAYER/CONFESSION

*O LORD of increase and abundance, I pray that You will be mindful of all the seeds of truth I have planted in my son/daughter. I pray these seeds will be watered by much love—both mine and Yours—and that they will germinate, grow and bring forth great increase in every area of his/her life. L*ORD *Jesus, just as You "increased" in wisdom, in stature and in favor with God and man, so let it be for my son/daughter. Yes, I pray, believe and confess that _____ will "increase with the increase of God"—in Jesus' Name, Amen (Let it be so)! (Colossians 2:19 KJV)*

26 *Strong Confidence*

In the fear of the LORD is strong confidence, and his
children shall have a place of refuge.   (Proverbs 14:26)

The Today's English Version of this passage explains, "Reverence for the LORD gives confidence and security to a man and his family." Many people lack confidence in life. Instead, they are intimidated by people, paralyzed by the past, perplexed by the present, afraid of the future and constantly battling insecurities and feelings of inferiority. Not so, for those who fear the LORD, for as the true maxim states—"The man or woman who fears God has nothing left to fear."

If we are submitted to the headship of Christ, "in Him we have boldness and access with confidence" (Ephesians 3:12). Most would concur this means "access" into the presence of the Father, but it may also mean "access" into our future destiny and purpose. Awakening in our offspring this kind of tenacious faith and bold assurance is very much a part of the spiritual legacy that we are called to impart.

PRAYER/CONFESSION

LORD GOD, first I claim an atmosphere of "the fear of the LORD"
permeating my home and hovering over my family—a loving
devotion that trembles at Your holiness, bows before Your majesty
and melts in Your presence. I declare that You are LORD of this home,
honoring You and reverencing You to the highest degree. I pray this
heart attitude of "the fear of the LORD" will always abide within
my child, and that as a result _____ will walk in strong
confidence all the days of his/her life. I confess that he/she will
never be intimidated by people, afraid of circumstances or
overwhelmed by challenges. Instead, may _____
always have a sense of unfailing security in You and in
the grace that You provide—in Jesus' Name,
Amen (Let it be so)!

27 A Place of Refuge

In the fear of the LORD is strong confidence, and his children shall have a place of refuge. (Proverbs 14:26)

The fear of the LORD is the highest degree of reverence for God and awe-filled devotion to Him. Parents whose hearts are inclined this way build a refuge for their children in a world that often disrespects and disregards who God is and what He wants of us. When we infuse our children's minds with the fear of the LORD, we position them in a place of accountability toward God and we awaken in them a desire to be acceptable in His sight. This builds confidence in our offspring: confidence that they can be right in God's sight, and qualify to receive His provision and protection.

We know ominous clouds are on the horizon spiritually. Very dark things are predicted over this planet. Such prophetic insight can cause even believers to be concerned about what their children might face. Yet we know that our Savior is "a refuge from the storm" (Isaiah 25:4). Though tumultuous times are ahead, the Prince of peace will come and make wars—"cease to the ends of the earth." No wonder the psalmist rejoicingly concluded, "The LORD of hosts is with us! The God of Jacob is our REFUGE" (Psalms 46:9, 11). No better refuge can be found!

PRAYER/CONFESSION

LORD GOD, I declare that I fear You, and I have endeavored to instill this worshipful and reverential awe in my child. We honor You and exalt You to the highest place in our lives. We are filled with awe at Your greatness, Your holiness and Your power. Because of this, I believe You will respond by building a wall of defense around us. I claim divine protection for my son/daughter in every area of life, especially as we approach "the last days." Though this world is filled with danger and deception, I confess that _____ will always have "a place of refuge" in You—in Jesus' Name, Amen (Let it be so)!

28 Freedom from Captivity

"Now it shall come to pass, when all these things come upon you, the blessing and the curse which I have set before you, and you call them to mind among all the nations where the LORD your God drives you,

And you return to the LORD your God and obey His voice, according to all that I command you today, you and your children, with all your heart and with all your soul;

That the LORD your God will bring you back from captivity, and have compassion on you, and gather you again from all the nations where the LORD your God has scattered you." (Deuteronomy 30:1-3)

On a New Covenant level, this promise is especially for families who have fallen away from the LORD, yet have repented and returned to Him. God pledges to deliver them from "captivity"—loosing them from the error of their past. However, this is not just for the formerly backslidden. We can all relate to this promise—for at times, we all "fall away" from the goal of walking in perfect faith, obedience and love. As a result, we become "captivated" by fear, doubt, depression, anger, resentment and many other kinds of bondage. But Jesus came to "proclaim liberty to the captives" (Isaiah 61:1).

The great mystery of the matter is this—having conquered the great enemies of the human race (sin, Satan, the curse, death and the grave) the Son of God ascended victoriously to heaven. During that pivotal event, this Captain of our salvation "led captivity captive" (Ephesians 4:8). In other words, He captivated, or put under His dominion, anything that could potentially captivate us, or our children. The more we return to the LORD—dedicating ourselves to the things of God—the more He will activate this part of our inheritance and loose us from any captivating influence.

LORD GOD, who bought our freedom through Your death, burial and resurrection, I recommit myself and my child to You. We have strayed from Your perfect will, at times, through our attitudes and actions, and ended up in some kind of captivity. I repent for myself and for _____ . I pray You will have compassion on us and deliver us from every area of bondage. I fully expect that You will do these things because You paid such an awesome price to set us free. Now it is our privilege and responsibility to respond. Through the weapons of warfare that You have given us, we even bring "every thought into captivity to the obedience of Christ." I refuse to accept any stronghold of negative or worldly thinking in me or in _____ . I claim the blood of Jesus, the Name of the LORD and the Word of God—weapons that are "mighty through God"— toppling every area of resistance in both of us. As the Scripture declares, "Evil people will surely be punished, but the children of the godly will go FREE." I claim that freedom in our family —in Jesus' Name, Amen (Let it be so)!

(Proverbs 11:21 NLT)

29 Compassion

"Now it shall come to pass, when all these things come upon you, the blessing and the curse which I have set before you, and you call them to mind among all the nations where the LORD your God drives you,

And you return to the LORD your God and obey His voice, according to all that I command you today, you and your children, with all your heart and with all your soul,

That the LORD your God will bring you back from captivity, and have compassion on you, and gather you again from all the nations where the LORD your God has scattered you." (Deuteronomy 30:1-3)

Compassion is sympathetic love—love that feels the pain of another person. We have all faltered and failed in life, and suffered the consequences. But according to this verse, if we return to God, He will have compassion on us and on our children.

The God of Abraham also promised that if His people "returned" to Him, they and their children would be "treated with compassion" by those who took them captive (2 Chronicles 30:9). One of the best examples is Pharaoh's daughter, who found the baby Moses in a basket floating down the Nile. "She had compassion on him" and he became her adopted son (Exodus 2:6). If this dual promise is given to erring, yet repentant believers, how much more will it manifest for those who are consistent in serving God!

PRAYER/CONFESSION

LORD GOD, I repent of all my shortcomings and areas of failure. I return to You with all of my heart and recommit myself to Your purpose. I believe You will honor Your Word, showing compassion to me and to my child _____ . I also believe that You will even cause others to show compassion toward us, because we are submitted to You—in Jesus' Name, Amen (Let it be so)!

30 *Doing Well*

"Therefore know this day, and consider it in your heart, that the LORD Himself is God in heaven above and on the earth beneath; there is no other.

You shall therefore keep His statutes and His commandments which I command you today, that it may go well with you and with your children after you, and that you may prolong your days in the land which the LORD your God is giving you for all time." (Deuteronomy 4:39-40)

A notable woman in Shunem who reverenced God offered the prophet Elisha a room in her home. God rewarded her with a miracle. Though childless, she conceived and bore a son. Later on, the child fell in the field crying, "My head" and died shortly after. The Shunammite rushed to find the man of God, expecting God to restore her child.

Gehazi, Elisha's servant, encountered the woman first and asked, "Is it well with you?…Is it well with the child?" Amazingly, her response was, "IT IS WELL" (2 Kings 4:19-37)! She dared to confess in advance what she believed God would do—and it happened. The child was raised back to life.

We should speak similar words of faith over our children, even if it appears they are nearly "dead" spiritually, or doing badly in certain areas. We should still dare to say, "IT IS WELL"—setting our faith in God's ability to change circumstance and to change hearts.

PRAYER/CONFESSION

LORD, I confess that You are God in heaven and on earth, and I seek to obey Your commandments. Therefore, I believe that it will "go well" with me and with my child _____, even as You promised, in every area of life. I believe this so utterly, that even in challenging or difficult times in my child's life, I dare to confess by faith "IT IS WELL!"—in Jesus' Name, Amen (Let it be so)!

31 Fearfully and Wonderfully Made

For You formed my inward parts; You covered me in my mother's womb.

I will praise You, for I am fearfully and wonderfully made; marvelous are Your works, and that my soul knows very well. (Psalms 139:13-14)

Unquestionably, the psalm containing this passage is one of David's most beautiful—a masterpiece of God-inspired truth. It celebrates God's involvement in the formation, both naturally and spiritually, of a child in the womb. Since the children of the righteous are usually consecrated to God prior to birth, the promises in this song of praise apply to them even more powerfully.

In the passage above, David claimed that the Most High actually formed his "inward parts." That could mean the organs of the body that are hidden from view, or it could mean the soul and spirit (the human personality and spiritual capacity of a child). Probably, it means both. So one of God's "marvelous works" is the implanting of a predetermined personality that must be perfected and a potential spirituality that must be awakened in a child that is yet to be born. As parents, we are called to assist in this process.

In the next two verses, David thrust his spiritual perception into a futuristic mode. Prayerfully he declared, "Your eyes saw my substance, being yet unformed. And in Your book they all were written, the days fashioned for me, when as yet there were none of them" (Psalms 139:15-16). So when a child is dedicated to God, there is a providential plan that unfolds like a huge red carpet, stretching all the way from the womb to the grave, then onward into eternity. Contemplating these promises should cause us to conclude, as David did—"such knowledge is too wonderful for me" (Psalms 139:6).

LORD GOD, I believe that my child has been "fearfully and wonderfully made." I confess that Your hand covered _____ in the womb and that Your hand will cover him/her all the days of his/her life. I believe that You have formed my child's "inward parts" (the potential personality and inner, spiritual capacity). I rest in this truth and pray that You will continue to involve Yourself in the soulish and spiritual development of my child, just as You involved Yourself in his/her physical development in the womb. Finally, I confess that the future of my child is not up to chance; You have a plan for _____ . I praise You for causing it to unfold perfectly according to Your pleasure. Such knowledge is so wonderful; it turns my heart upward in worship toward You, O LORD of the past, present and future. I declare victory in advance—in Jesus' Name, Amen (Let it be so)!

32   *Longevity*

"Today I am explaining His laws and teachings. And if you always obey them, you and your descendants will live long and be successful in the land the LORD is giving you."
(Deuteronomy 4:40 CEV)

Legend has it that Ponce de Leon discovered Florida in 1513 while seeking the "Fountain of Youth." Eight years later, instead of finding the key to longevity, he died at the hands of the Calusa Indians. Ironically, a search for extended life actually led to an early death.

Now, as the baby boomer generation moves into the status of "senior citizens," the search is still going on. A new industry is flourishing—the Science of Anti-Aging. By implementing nutritional and exercise principles, some may be able to temporarily fend off the grip of time, but eventually, all human beings will fall prey to this persistent stalker.

Thankfully, there is a refuge. Our key scripture reveals the importance of obeying God's commands. Other scriptures include:

(1) Honoring your father and mother, *"that your days may be long..."* (Exodus 20:12).

(2) Seeking wisdom, for *"length of days is in her right hand"* (Proverbs 3:16).

(3) Setting your love upon God and knowing His name, for He promises such a person, *"with long life I will satisfy him"* (Psalms 91:16).

(4) Rehearsing and displaying God's Word in the home, *"That your days and the days of your children may be multiplied...like the days of the heavens above the earth"* (Deuteronomy 11:18-21).

Of course, the most excellent promise is immortality—received by setting our faith on the LORD Jesus Christ, for "He who believes in the Son has EVERLASTING LIFE" (John 3:36).

LORD GOD, I make a commitment to obey Your commandments, to seek wisdom, to set my love upon You and to fill my home with Your Word—that my days, and the days of my child, may be long upon the earth. More importantly, I confess that my faith is set upon You, JESUS, that I might inherit the gift of eternal life. May this gift of all gifts also be poured out on my son/daughter, that _____ and I might live forever in Your presence. Amen (Let it be so)!

33   *Success*

*"Today I am explaining His laws and teachings. And if
you always obey them, you and your descendants will live
long and be successful in the land the* Lord *is giving you."*
(Deuteronomy 4:40 CEV)

Success seminars have abounded in recent years. Many "keys
to success" are celebrated: a good self-image, positive thinking, a
proper education, neatness of appearance, eloquence in speech,
showing genuine interest in others, calling people by their names,
and so forth. There is certainly some degree of worth in all these
points, but the most important issue is often left out.

God admonished Joshua, "This Book of the Law shall not
depart from your mouth, but you shall meditate in it day and
night, that you may observe to do according to all that is written
in it. For then you will make your way prosperous, and then you
will have *good success*" (Joshua 1:8, emphasis by author).

Daily confessing Scripture, pondering its true meaning,
keeping its commands and claiming its promises—these are some
of the greatest keys to success that exist—for us and for our
children. There is no greater way of describing the resulting legacy
than the New Living Translation of Psalms 112:1-2, "How joyful
are those who fear the Lord, and delight in obeying His commands.
Their children will be successful everywhere."

PRAYER/CONFESSION

*LORD GOD, I declare that I honor Your Word—that it will always
be "in my mouth." I will "meditate" on it day and night, and I will
always seek to live within its boundaries. I believe this will bring
"good success" in my own life and in the life of my son/daughter. I
now pass on this legacy of a Word-based lifestyle to _____ .
It will cause my child "to be successful everywhere" that
he/she goes—in Jesus' Name, Amen (Let it be so)!*

34 *Deliverance*

*Though hand join in hand, the wicked shall not be
unpunished: but the seed of the righteous shall be delivered.*
(Proverbs 11:21)

It was the first Passover in the land of Goshen. In the early
evening, thousands of Israeli men dipped hyssop in lamb's blood
and applied it to the upper doorpost and two side posts of their homes.
The destroyer would visit Egypt that night and the firstborn son of
every household would die. But God promised His people, "When I
see the blood, I will pass over you" (Exodus 12:13). The next day,
wails were heard all over the land—the Egyptian sons were slain
and great grief, like the waters of the swollen Nile, flowed through
the streets, lanes and alleys. But the Israelite sons were delivered.

The men of Israel had no idea that their action of applying
lamb's blood was prophetic in nature, that they were actually making
the sign of the cross—"prophesying" of another "Lamb" yet to come
who would deliver His people from death—not only physically,
but spiritually and eternally. In a way similar to this grand Biblical
event, we must mark our homes, claiming the blood of Jesus as a
protective covering over our seed. As many young people succumb
to the death-dealing influences of a society become increasingly
evil, it is our responsibility, as parents, to make a prayerful,
prophetic statement that heaven will honor.

PRAYER/CONFESSION

*LORD GOD, there are many death-dealing influences around my
child. The world system, dominated by the Evil One, has a soul-
destroying effect on children who are unprotected. But I claim the
blood of Jesus over my home and my offspring. I believe that
_____ will be preserved from evil for "the eye of the LORD is on
those…who hope in His mercy, to deliver their soul from death."
—in Jesus' Name, Amen (Let it be so)! (Psalms 33:19)*

35 *Foolishness Removed*

Foolishness is bound up in the heart of a child; the rod of correction will drive it far from him.   (Proverbs 22:15)

Most Bible promises are attached to conditions. This is a prime example. In order for foolishness to be driven from the hearts of our children, we must be willing to wield "the rod of correction"—but what is that *rod*? Is it just physical punishment for shortcomings? That may certainly part of it (as the old adage goes, "Spare the rod and spoil the child"—See Proverbs 23:14).

Sometimes, though, a rod can represent words—especially words spoken with authority. A good example is Isaiah 11:4—a prophecy that the Messiah would "strike the earth with the rod of His mouth." (Isaiah 11:4, See Proverbs 14:3.) Jesus was no easy-going preacher; He exposed hypocrisy, sin and rebellion whenever He preached.

Those who love God welcome His words of correction, for they keep us from the contaminating influence of a foolish world. In the end, our children will love us also, if we are careful to discipline them this way: correcting wrong behavior and leading them in the path of wisdom. David, in his famed 23rd Psalm, told the Shepherd-God, "Your *rod* and your staff comfort me" (Psalms 23:4). Similarly, the "rod of correction" wielded by loving parents should also be a "comfort" to any child—for their words point the way to a life that pleases God.

LORD GOD, how foolish this world is with its ungodly agendas and its refusal to surrender to the truth. Your Word says that even the "thought of foolishness is sin." I repent of it all. I ask You to cleanse me and my child of all worldly influence. I recognize that "foolishness" is "bound up" in the heart of my child, because of an inherited fallen nature. But Your Word can remove it and drive it far from him/her. I pray that _____ will not succumb to the foolishness of the carnal nature, but will instead embrace the wisdom of God and receive a new nature. I make a commitment to lovingly discipline my child when it is needed, so that the "rod of my mouth" will lead him/her in the way of truth and bring comfort to my child, now and forevermore—in Jesus' Name, Amen (Let it be so)! (Proverbs 24:9)

36 Rooted in the Truth

*Train up a child in the way he should go, and when he
is old he will not depart from it.* (Proverbs 22:6)

Years ago, I visited a friend whose hobby was horticultural
studies (a step above mere gardening). At the entrance of his home
was a small tree I didn't recognize. "What's that?" I questioned. "A
weeping cherry tree," he responded. Surprised, I said, "I've heard of
a weeping willow, but not a weeping cherry tree. Don't the branches
of a cherry tree grow straight up? But these are hanging down."

Larry then proceeded to explain how he did it. When the tree
was just a sapling, he split the trunk, turned one side upside down,
then fused the two pieces back together. He explained that this
confused the tree's "internal thinking," so that later on, when it
"thought" it was "growing up," it was really "growing down."

That happens with children too. Sometimes through the bad
influence of carnal-minded, worldly-living parents or authority
figures, they get "twisted" around in their thinking at an early age.
Consequently, they often equate "adulthood" with sensual
indulgence and sinful excess. As they get older, they tend to mimic
the same behavior. However, when they think that they are finally
"growing up," in reality, they are "growing down."

Of course, if the negative is true, the positive is true also. Good
role models persist for a lifetime. Parents who live a life of goodness
and morality are "training" by example. They are guarding their
offspring with a lasting impression of the truth that will cause little
"saplings" to grow up healthy and normal. Yes, we need to "train"
the minds of our children in Biblical truths and moral laws, but better
than that, we need to live those truths and laws before their
impressionable eyes every day.

PRAYER/CONFESSION

LORD GOD, when You came to earth, You "trained" us by sharing many truth-concepts that challenge the world's way of doing things. But better than that, You lived out those concepts before us. Help me to properly train my child, not only in words, but with my example. Then, let both leave a lasting impression on my child's heart and mind, so that when _____ is grown, he/she will not depart from the right way of living. I claim this promise and expect it to come to pass— in Jesus' Name, Amen (Let it be so)!

37 Preserved from Trouble

"They shall not labor in vain, nor bring forth children for trouble; for they shall be the descendants of the blessed of the Lord, and their offspring with them." (Isaiah 65:23)

When taken in context, it is clear that this verse foretells the glory of the New Creation. God also promises that He will create Jerusalem "a rejoicing and her people a joy." No longer will "the voice of weeping" be heard. Life will be stable. God's elect will "long enjoy the work of their hands." All of nature will be reconciled: for "the wolf and the lamb shall feed together." The land will be called "Beulah," meaning married—for all things will be married to God in an overflow of celestial splendor. (See Isaiah 62:4; 65:18-25.)

The Holy Spirit also foretells that the people of the New Earth will not "labor in vain, nor bring forth children for trouble" for they are "the seed of the blessed of the Lord, and their offspring with them" (Isaiah 65:23 NKJV, KJV). Though this promise is primarily futuristic, the "blessed of the Lord" can confess even now, "I did not bring my child into this world for trouble, to be overcome by trials, temptations or tribulations. By faith, I declare that he/she will have a peaceful, fruitful and successful life."

PRAYER/CONFESSION

LORD, I confess that I did not bring _____ into this world to be destroyed by the troubling things that abound here. As a family we may face temptations and trials, but we know You will be our "strength in the time of trouble," a "refuge in the time of trouble" and will even "preserve" us "from trouble." I declare by faith, in the end, that any troublesome thing encountered in life will only serve to help God's purposes achieve final fulfillment—in Jesus' Name, Amen (Let it be so)! (Psalms 9:9; 32:7; 37:39, See Proverbs 11:8; 12:13.)

38 Providential Care

"They shall not labor in vain, nor bring forth children for trouble; for they shall be the descendants of the blessed of the LORD, and their offspring with them.

It shall come to pass that before they call, I will answer; and while they are still speaking, I will hear."

(Isaiah 65:23-24)

On the highest level, this passage of Scripture prophesies of the glorious reign of Jesus Christ in the new world which is yet to come. In that era, God will be so intimately involved with His people, that He will automatically anticipate anything they might request of Him. In one version, God says, "I will answer their prayers before they finish praying" (CEV). That's just the way a loving Father is.

Of course, good parents do something similar just about every day. A concerned mother knows when she picks up her daughter from school, she's going to want her favorite snack, so she prepares in advance. As soon as that girl says, "Mommy...," the mother interrupts, "It's in the bag next to you"—and the broad smile breaks. If earthly parents can be that way with their offspring, how much more the omniscient, omnipotent, omnipresent God! He knows what we need before we do. Such compassionate oversight is not just futuristic in the Kingdom to come; it is a present promise that both we and our offspring can claim right now.

PRAYER/CONFESSION

LORD GOD, I confess that my child and I are blessed and that You are watching over us constantly—ever anticipating our future needs. You promised that before we call upon You, the answer will be sent. I claim that kind of divine oversight for my son/daughter. May _____ never face anything in life without Your grace and provision being supplied ahead of time and manifesting right when it is needed—in Jesus' Name, Amen (Let it be so)! (Ephesians 1:4)

39 Vessels of Perfect Praise

> *But when the chief priests and scribes saw the wonderful things that He did, and the children crying out in the temple and saying, "Hosanna to the Son of David!" they were indignant,*
>
> *And said to Him, "Do You hear what these are saying?" And Jesus said to them, "Yes. Have you never read, 'Out of the mouth of babes and nursing infants You have perfected praise'?"*   (Matthew 21:15-16)

After Jesus cleansed the temple of the moneychangers, the blind and lame came to Him and were healed. The children present began worshipping the LORD, shouting, "Hosanna to the Son of David!" This greatly offended the religious leaders who were steeped in their own self-importance and self-righteousness. Jesus responded to them by quoting this verse from Psalm 8.

It is quite amazing that such top-rated theologians of Jesus' day were so oblivious to the power of God manifesting before their eyes—but tragically, they were. On the other hand, the children were not blinded by traditions and doctrines. They were not nervously protecting some political or ecclesiastical position of power. They were just ecstatic at what God was doing and willing to respond with joy. Far too often, the praise that goes on in our churches is linked to mindless ritual, tainted by religious pride and devoid of passion.

Real praise is not practiced, polished, professional or performed. It is simple, sincere, humble, heartfelt, spontaneous and full of passion toward the Most High. Jesus claimed that God perfects this kind of praise in children.

PRAYER/CONFESSION

LORD GOD, You deserve to be praised with all our heart, mind, soul and strength. I pray that You will awaken this in _____, that You will make him/her a true vessel of praise. May _____ always react to the blessings of God with great gratitude and a river of heartfelt adoration flowing upward to Your throne. Yes, LORD, I confess that my son/daughter will be a true worshipper all the days of his/her life— in Jesus' Name, Amen (Let it be so)!

40 Continuance

The children of Your servants will continue, and their descendants will be established before You. (Psalms 102:28)

On the first level, this speaks of the physical continuation of the family line from generation to generation—a family that survives. On the second level, it speaks of an attitude of heart. Especially in this era, so many people lack consistency and diligence, sticking with a task until it's done, hanging in there when the going gets tough. But in this verse God promises His servants that their offspring will be quite the opposite. Why?

Often the attitude is inherited. When children witness contagious stick-to-itiveness in their parents, they tend to "catch it." Most godly people have plenty of trials to pass through, but if they are truly committed, they do just that—they pass through. They keep going. The Bible urges God's people to "continue in the faith," "continue in the grace of God," "continue in His goodness" and "continue earnestly in prayer" (Acts 13:43; 14:22, Romans 11:22, Colossians 4:2). Jesus summed it up with the challenge, "If you continue in My Word, you are My disciples indeed!" (John 8:31 MKJV). Let these Bible passages be descriptive of you, and of your child as well.

PRAYER/CONFESSION

LORD GOD, You are the unchanging God; You remain the same yesterday, today and forever. I pray that You will so infuse my family with Your nature that we also never change—in our commitment to the truth. Give me grace first, as a parent, to continue in Your Word— always abiding by its commands and promises. Then second, let this legacy pass to my child. I pray that _____ will be consistent in his/her relationship with You, that he/she will continue in the faith, continue in the grace of God, continue in Your goodness, and continue in earnest prayerfulness—in Jesus' Name, Amen (Let it be so)!

41 Stability

The children of Your servants will continue, and their descendants will be established before You. (Psalms 102:28)

To be "established" means to be made firm or stable. This world is quite the opposite: a very unpredictable, unstable place. One day everything can be wonderful, and the next day, disaster can strike. Notable events from the past easily prove this: Black Tuesday, Pearl Harbor, 9/11, Hurricane Katrina—just to mention a few. But no matter what happens, those who walk with God can be steady...unafraid...undeterred concerning their purpose.

Many promises in Scripture confirm this. One stands out—"But the LORD is faithful, who will establish you and guard you from the evil one" (2 Thessalonians 3:3). In this passage, the mystery is unveiled. We can expect stability in our lives and the lives of our children, simply because God is stable. He is unchanging—faithful to the principles that rule His Kingdom, faithful to those who love Him and faithful to their offspring. Our seed are "established *before* God." Being under His constant surveillance, He is always ready to intervene in their behalf.

PRAYER/CONFESSION

LORD GOD, I thank You for showing me the source of stability in this unpredictable world. I declare over my household that "God is our refuge and strength, a very present help in trouble. Therefore we will not fear, though the earth be removed, and though the mountains be carried into the midst of the sea." Yes, even in times of cataclysmic upheaval, we can trust in You and be unmoved. I claim this kind of stability for myself and for my child, _____ . I believe You will "establish peace for us," "establish the work of our hands" and finally, establish our "hearts blameless in holiness before our God...at the coming of our LORD Jesus Christ." Amen (Let it be so)!
(Psalms 46:1-2; 90:17, Isaiah 26:12, 1 Thessalonians 3:13)

42 Spiritual Might

Praise the LORD! Blessed is the man who fears the LORD,
who delights greatly in His commandments.
His descendants will be mighty on earth; the generation
of the upright will be blessed. (Psalms 112:1-2)

This is a power-promise if there ever was one. Weak parents tend to raise weak children. But parents who fear the LORD—that's another story! By yielding to God's Spirit (called the "Spirit of might" in Isaiah 11:2), they conquer sin, they conquer self and they conquer the spirit of the world. What a legacy to pass on! The children of such parents know, "If Dad and Mom can overcome that way, I can too!" Thus, they are far more capable at doing mighty things in life and impacting the world in a mighty way.

Orville and Wilbur Wright had strong Christian parents and look at how mightily they have influenced the earth—through the development of air flight over the past 100 years. And what about Billy Graham, inarguably one of the most influential Christian leaders of this generation? He had strong Christian parents. After receiving the baton of consecrated faith from them, he passed it on to his offspring as well, and they are still mightily impacting this world with the Gospel. May the same thing take place in your family!

PRAYER/CONFESSION

LORD, I live before You in godly fear: reverence for Your holiness, and awe of Your majesty and power. My passion is to keep Your commandments. I delight in obeying Your Word. So, according to this promise, I can expect my son/daughter to do mighty works for the Kingdom of God and change this world in a mighty way. Father, I pray You will awaken the "Spirit of might" in _____ and strengthen him/her with "might" through Your Spirit "in the inner man"—in Jesus' Name, Amen (Let it be so)! (Ephesians 3:16)

43 Wealth

Praise the LORD! Blessed is the man who fears the LORD, who delights greatly in His commandments.

His descendants will be mighty on earth; the generation of the upright will be blessed.

Wealth and riches will be in his house, and his righteousness endures forever. (Psalms 112:1-3)

The Good News translation of this passage says, "Happy is the person who honors the LORD, who takes pleasure in obeying His commands. The good man's children will be powerful in the land; his descendants will be blessed. His family will be wealthy and rich."

Sought for its own sake, wealth can be corruptive, but sought for the Kingdom's sake, it can be very beneficial. When God sees that our priorities are right, pouring out power, wealth, riches, prosperity and success is something He desires to do—for us and for our children.

Deuteronomy 8:18 reveals the primary reason God gives the seed of the righteous "power to get wealth." He does so that He may "establish" the covenant made with their foreparents. So if we serve God there should be an overflow in this area to our children. As the puritan preacher, Cotton Mather, put it, "Religion begets prosperity."

The Almighty knows that His work requires financing: churches must be built, missionaries must be supported, television and radio programs must be produced, books and tracts must be published and the poor must be given much-needed assistance. To accomplish these worthy goals, the LORD of all empowers certain individuals in the body of Christ to prosper materially, then passes the same blessing on to their offspring. Like Abraham of old, they are "blessed" to "be a blessing" (Genesis 12:2).

LORD GOD of heaven and earth, I confess that all the earth is Yours and the fullness of it. All the silver is Yours and all the gold. All the cattle on a thousand hills belong to You. So I claim this promise of wealth for my son/daughter, but not just for his/her benefit personally. More importantly, I claim this promise so that _____ will be used by You, LORD, to finance Your work and the great harvest of souls that will surely take place in these last days. I also pray, LORD God, that wealth will never corrupt my child, but that on the contrary, he/she will always seek the "wealth" of Your people, just as Mordecai did so many years ago. Once this blessings manifests, may _____ always be minded toward helping the poor and underprivileged—for this is the heart of God—in Jesus' Name, Amen (Let it be so)!
(Esther 10:3 KJV, MKJV)

44 *Riches*

Praise the LORD! Blessed is the man who fears the LORD, who delights greatly in His commandments.

His descendants will be mighty on earth; the generation of the upright will be blessed.

Wealth and riches will be in his house, and his righteousness endures forever. (Psalms 112:1-3)

The word "house" refers to a person's household or family. Accordingly, the Good News translation renders this passage—"The good man's children will be powerful in the land; his descendents will be blessed. His family will be wealthy and rich..."

There is plenty of evidence that material riches are, at times, very much a part of God's blessing. For example, Abraham was "VERY RICH in livestock, in silver, and in gold" (Genesis 13:2). Along with his far-more-important spiritual legacy, natural riches were part of the inheritance Abraham passed to His offspring. It is also true that many centuries later Jesus actually became "a curse" (when he died on the cross) so "the blessing of Abraham" could pass to all New Covenant children of God (Galatians 3:13-14).

Of course, the greatest "riches" are spiritual in nature. Jesus called them "true riches" (Luke 16:11). God has promised that His people will inherit the riches of His goodness, the riches of His mercy, the riches of His grace and the riches of His glory (Romans 2:4; 9:23, Ephesians 1:7; 2:4). Furthermore, James 2:5 asks, "Has not God chosen the poor of this world to be rich in faith and heirs of the Kingdom which He promised to those who love Him?" These are the primary riches that we should all desire, but both classes of riches—natural and spiritual—are part of the dual legacy that we can pass to our children.

LORD GOD of the entire universe, all things belong to You. In Your abundant generosity, You have promised to meet all our needs according to Your riches in glory. I pray first for _____ that the Word of God will dwell in him/her richly, and that he/she will be filled with the riches of Your mercy, Your goodness and Your grace. I believe that _____ will not only be rich in faith, but rich in good works, as the Scripture commands. I also claim natural riches for my child, but not to the detriment of his/her relationship with You. Let riches increase in his/her life, but let love for God and spirituality increase even more, so that my child, above all, is "rich toward God." Since I believe You have already purposed to do this, by faith, I confess over _____ the words of 1 Corinthians 4:8, "NOW YOU ARE RICH…"—in Jesus' Name, Amen (Let it be so)! (Luke 12:21, See 1 Timothy 6:18.)

45 *Redemption*

> *"The LORD did not set His love on you nor choose you because you were more in number than any other people, for you were the least of all peoples;*
>
> *But because the LORD loves you, and because He would keep the oath which He swore to your fathers, the LORD has brought you out with a mighty hand, and redeemed you from the house of bondage, from the hand of Pharaoh king of Egypt."*
>
> (Deuteronomy 7:7-8)

To be redeemed means to be loosed away from bondage by means of a purchase price. In this passage God promises redemption to the Israelite people on the basis of the oath that He swore to their forefathers. If we are in a covenant relationship with the same God, we can expect similar treatment for our offspring as well, yet in a much higher sense. No matter what "bondage" may be in their lives, we can prayerfully confess that God will redeem them and bring them out with "a mighty hand." Therefore, "let the redeemed of the LORD say so" (Psalms 107:2)!

PRAYER/CONFESSION

LORD GOD, I confess that my son/daughter is loosed from all bondage—redeemed, liberated, set free by the precious blood of Jesus. No past, present or future bondage will ever prevail against _____ . The world, sin, deception, satanic enticements, the nature of the flesh, even fear of death—none of these things will ever be able to enslave this child who is dedicated to You. I pray that You will always be a Redeemer, Deliverer, Guardian and Guide to _____ bringing him/her out of any weakness, any darkness or any difficult situation of life. By Your MIGHTY hand, I pray You will lead my child into the Promised Land of his/her destiny. You are the ALMIGHTY GOD! There is nothing too hard for You! So I declare redemption over my offspring, believing it will come to pass—in Jesus' Name, Amen (Let it be so)!

46 Prophetic Insights

"And it shall come to pass in the last days," says God, "that I will pour out of My Spirit on all flesh; your sons and your daughters shall prophesy, your young men shall see visions, your old men shall dream dreams." (Acts 2:17)

This prophecy (originally given in Joel 2:28) began its era of fulfillment with the birth of the church on Pentecost. (See Acts 2: 1-18.) It is still coming to pass, for God is still pouring out His Spirit on sons and daughters and transforming them into prophets and prophetesses of the LORD. Such terminology sounds a little presumptuous to some believers, yet it is very Biblical.

Prophetic insights can manifest on several levels. On the most fundamental level, a person can be described as "prophesying" when he or she simply shares the Word of God under the power, guidance and inspiration of the Holy Spirit (sensing who to speak to, what to say, and when to say it). This can happen standing in a pulpit, talking with a neighbor over a back yard fence or even in the face of opposition. (See Matthew 10:20.)

At times, God speaks to His people in prophetic words, dreams or visions—granting them insights concerning certain people or events, or their own destiny in God. (See Numbers 12:6, John 10:27.)

Prophetic knowledge is especially associated with those who have inspired "glimpses" into the future of God's purposes in the earth. Anyone who can read the Bible has some access to this kind of information in its simplest form, but only born again, consecrated individuals can interpret and propagate the message properly—through the power of the Holy Spirit. Anyone who is truly saved can be used this way. "You may all prophesy," Paul asserted—and that includes you and your offspring who are walking with God (1 Corinthians 14:31).

PRAYER/CONFESSION

LORD GOD Almighty, I pray that according to the promise of Acts 2:17, You will pour out Your Spirit on _____ and awaken a prophetic calling and gift in his/her life. Thank you for manifesting prophetic knowledge in _____ on several levels: first, that he/she will understand Your Word by divine inspiration; second, that he/she will be able to effectively prophesy truth to others by the power and inspiration of the Holy Spirit; and third, that he/she will have great insights into the unfolding of prophetic events in the last days as we near Your return. I pray that You will grant _____ prophetic words, dreams and visions, and give my child grace to boldly proclaim what he/she receives from you. I confess that these things will happen, all for Your glory and the advancement of Your Kingdom—in Jesus' Name, Amen (Let it be so)!

47 *Visions*

"And it shall come to pass in the last days," says God, "that I will pour out of My Spirit on all flesh; your sons and your daughters shall prophesy, your young men shall see visions, your old men shall dream dreams." (Acts 2:17)

Visionaries are those who receive plans, strategies and purposes from God. By faith and by God's power they implement those divine instructions to advance the Kingdom of God in this world. Every generation needs "seers"—people of vision who know, by divine inspiration, exactly what to do order to impact individuals, communities, or even nations, significantly for the Gospel's sake. There is absolutely no reason why such a status should be reserved to adults alone. This verse promises literal "visions" from God to our sons, and surely, our daughters as well. At an early age, Samuel received a vision from God that altered his life dramatically and caused him to emerge as a prophet to his generation.

God still moves on children supernaturally. Sometimes they even receive literal "visions" from the Almighty. When our son was only about four years old, one morning, he surprised us all by blurting out, "Last night I died in my sleep and Jesus took me to heaven!" Then he began to explain certain details about what he heard and saw. The descriptions were so profoundly deep and the language so mature, we knew it could not be the mere product of a child's imagination. Though he certainly didn't "die," we believe he definitely experienced a night-vision from the LORD, a grace-filled glimpse of the celestial world.

May God grant your child supernatural visitations as well!

LORD GOD Almighty, I confess this promise of vision over my son/daughter. Thank you for pouring out Your Spirit on _____ and supernaturally revealing Your plans for his/her life. Then, I pray You will cause my child's heart to burn with passionate commitment to the holy cause that You place within him/her. Holy Father, I believe You will open my son's/daughter's spiritual sight, even to the point of receiving actual "visions" from above, as You did for Samuel when he was a child. I pray that _____ will never accept a mundane and normal life, but will reach out with visionary zeal to embrace the uncommon and God-inspired goals that are a part of Your plan. On the basis of this promise in Acts 2:17, I claim both waking visions and night visions (inspired dreams) for my child, that he/she might be led into the depth of Your purpose, and that he/she might be a champion for the truth in this world—in Jesus' Name, Amen (Let it be so)!

48 *Power to Stand*

The wicked are overthrown and are no more, but the house of the righteous will stand. (Proverbs 12:7)

This verse speaks of two primary things. First, it implies that a life of righteousness tends to bring stability and long-term growth to a family—the "house" as a whole will stand.

Second, this verse speaks God's promise to the individual offspring—that in times of trouble, times of disappointment, times of lack, and even times of oppression and persecution—the seed of the righteous will "stand." They will not back down, give up or waver. The white flag of surrender is not in their survival kit. They will stand fast, resisting temptation and possessing their God-given inheritance.

This is part of the legacy godly fathers and mothers pass down. When the children of the righteous watch their parents go through tough times—and watch them survive by fighting the good fight of faith and seizing God's promises—they learn to imitate the same tenacious behavior. Example engenders the same in their hearts, and the family tradition continues.

PRAYER/CONFESSION

LORD GOD, I believe that my child will stand firm, trusting in the promises of God, no matter what he/she faces in life. I confess that _____ will stand against temptation when it entices, stand for the truth when others compromise, and stand in faith when circumstances cause clouds of doubt to overshadow his/her mind. I pray _____ will be a worshipper and "stand in Your holy place." I pray _____ will be an intercessor and "stand in the gap" for others. Finally, I pray that _____ will never be intimidated by fearful things in life, but will instead "stand still" and see the salvation of the LORD—in Jesus' Name, Amen (Let it be so)!
(Psalms 24:3, Ezekiel 22:30, Exodus 14:13)

49 *Divine Health*

Because you have made the LORD, who is my refuge,
even the Most High, your dwelling place,
No evil shall befall you, nor shall any plague come near
your dwelling. (Psalms 91:9-10)

What does it mean to make the LORD your "dwelling place"? Surely that is much different than just visiting Him in times of trouble (getting religious when the heat's on). Rather, it speaks of a 24/7 relationship, having a heart that is always inclined toward heaven.

When God finds such quality souls, He promises the reward found in our key scripture. In essence, He is saying, "If you make the decision to live with Me, then I will make the decision to live with you. I will be an invisible Presence, abiding in your home, repelling evil and pouring out My blessing on all who live under your roof."

The specific promise mentioned is divine health: not just the removal of disease, but the prevention of it. It will not come "near" our "dwelling." Those who live in our homes (especially our children) should automatically get the "overflow" of this blessing. If Obed-Edom's household was blessed, just because the Ark of Covenant was placed in his home, how much MORE will your household be blessed—if the One the Ark symbolized abides among you. (See 2 Samuel 6:11.)

PRAYER/CONFESSION

LORD GOD, I believe the promise of Deuteronomy 7:15, that You will
"take away all sickness" from Your people—but better than that, I
believe the promise of Psalm 91:10, that no sickness can come near my
dwelling. I confess that You are a refuge for me and for my son/
daughter. Thank You for protecting _____ from all disease and
imparting divine health to our family—wholeness in body, mind, soul
and spirit. You are "THE LORD OUR HEALER" and You are LORD of
our home—in Jesus' Name, Amen (Let it be so)! (Exodus 15:26)

50 Knowing God's Word

For He established a testimony in Jacob, and appointed a law in Israel, which He commanded our fathers, that they should make them known to their children;

That the generation to come might know them, the children who would be born, that they may arise and declare them to their children. (Psalms 78:5-6)

The word translated "law" in this passage is the Hebrew word *Torah*. This is actually a name for the first five books of the Bible: Genesis, Exodus, Leviticus, Numbers and Deuteronomy. These contain much more than just "the law" (a list of commandments from God). These foundational books are full of faith-building stories, wonderful revelations of the character of God and prophetic glimpses of what is yet to come. We have more than five books now; we have sixty-six. How much more valuable is this treasure now, especially those books revealing the life of Jesus and the glory of the New Covenant!

It is very important that this knowledge be imparted to the next generation. We cannot keep it to ourselves. Thank God for those who have diligently watched over the preservation of God's Word in centuries past—like the scribes of old who carefully handwrote God's Word one copy at a time—or more recent heroes, like Wycliffe and Tyndale, who first dared to translate the Bible from Latin into English, the language of the common people. Tyndale was martyred for his "crime." May we value the price that others have paid, cherish God's Word, promote it in all that we do, preserve its values and pass this holy responsibility on to our seed—that the work of God might continue in the earth.

LORD GOD, Your Word is a lamp unto our feet and a light unto our path. This is such a dark world, full of deception and death. There are no survivors here except those who discover Your truth and live in it. Help me to transfer to my offspring the correct interpretation of Your Word and awaken in _____ a deep understanding of truth and a deep appreciation of its value. Help me to live your Word before my child so that he/she receives a living example of how the Word of God should mold our lives, then empower _____ to walk in my footsteps and be a testimony of truth to the next generation—in Jesus' Name, Amen (Let it be so)!

51 Hope in God

For He established a testimony in Jacob, and appointed a law in Israel, which He commanded our fathers, that they should make them known to their children;

That the generation to come might know them, the children who would be born, that they may arise and declare them to their children,

That they may set their hope in God, and not forget the works of God, but keep His commandments. (Psalms 78:5-7)

Hope has been defined as *desire married to expectation.* Tertullian, one of the early church fathers, said, *"Hope is patience with the lamp lit."* According to our key passage, one of the primary reasons God gave us His Word was to transfer "hope" to future generations. It is not enough for this soul-warming sunshine to reach the full-grown "trees"; it must shine down to the forest floor and nurture the "saplings" as well.

Life is often unpredictable. At times we may even face what appears to be a hopeless situation—but we are in covenant with the "God of hope" who fills us with "all joy and peace in believing" that we may "abound in hope by the power of the Holy Spirit" (Romans 15:13).

Though this generation is careening downhill toward a time of great tribulation as the world has never seen, we have a "blessed hope": the glorious appearing of the LORD Jesus Christ. The Scripture promises, when we see Him, "we shall be like Him" and that "everyone who has this HOPE in him purifies himself, just as He is pure" (Titus 2:13, 1 John 3:2-3). Yes, of all the promises we can pass to our children this is one of the most important—that Jesus is coming again to establish Himself once and for all as LORD of lords and KING of kings—in heaven and on earth!

LORD, I set my hope in You—always and in all things. I declare that there is no hopeless situation. Thank You for giving me the courage to expect Your promises to be fulfilled. This hope is the "anchor" of my soul in stormy seas. By faith, I pass this spiritual capacity to my child: the ability to hold on tenaciously to the promises of God, no matter what happens in life. I believe that You will fill _____ with "all joy and peace in believing" that he/she may always "abound in hope" through the power of the Holy Spirit, as we both look forward to that "blessed hope" of Your return, and " the hope of glory" that resides within us
—in Jesus' Name, Amen (Let it be so)!
(See Hebrews 6:17-20, Colossians 1:27.)

52 Remembering God's Works

For He established a testimony in Jacob, and appointed a law in Israel, which He commanded our fathers, that they should make them known to their children;

That the generation to come might know them, the children who would be born, that they may arise and declare them to their children,

That they may set their hope in God, and not forget the works of God, but keep His commandments. (Psalms 78:5-7)

Sharing the Word of God with our children prepares them for life. As we tell the story of Adam and Eve, they will understand our fallen state and God's promise of redemption. When they hear of Noah and his family, they will understand that God protects His own. As we tell of Abraham and Sarah, faith can be built in them for overcoming impossible situations. As we relate the deliverance of Israel from Egypt, they will be convinced God's power can set them free from any bondage in their lives.

It is so important to impart this knowledge. After the Israelites passed over Jordan and possessed the Land of Promise, a horrible thing transpired. Judges 2:11-12 relates, "When all that generation had been gathered to their fathers, another generation arose after them who did not know the LORD nor the work which He had done for Israel. Then the children of Israel did evil in the sight of the LORD…and they forsook the LORD God of their fathers…." This must not take place in your family. Reach back in your memory banks and think of all the "works of God" you have witnessed in your own life personally. Share these stories with your child—often. By doing so, you will keep the fire burning, that it might continue shining brightly, from generation to generation.

LORD GOD ALMIGHTY, I praise You for all Your mighty works—
those You have accomplished in generations past, and those You have
wrought during my lifetime. Give me grace to transfer to my child,
not only the knowledge of these works—but the expectation that You
can move in his/her behalf as well. Don't ever let my child forget
what You have done. I claim the ever constant overshadowing
of the "Spirit of truth" upon _____ bringing all
of God's works and God's Word to his/her remembrance, that
he/she might serve You and be kept from this evil world—
in Jesus' Name, Amen (Let it be so)!
(John 14:17, 26)

53 Keeping God's Commandments

For He established a testimony in Jacob, and appointed a law in Israel, which He commanded our fathers, that they should make them known to their children;

That the generation to come might know them, the children who would be born, that they may arise and declare them to their children,

That they may set their hope in God, and not forget the works of God, but keep His commandments. (Psalms 78:5-7)

The only way to live a life of complete obedience to God is to know His commandments. The Hebrew word translated "law" in verse five is *Torah*—a word that refers to the first five books of the Bible. Traditionally, the Torah is said to contain 613 commandments (365 negative commandments and 248 affirmative ones). Not all of these are required of God's people now, because of the coming of Jesus and the fulfilling of the law. However, we are not without law. The Bible says we are "under the law to Christ" (1 Corinthians 9:21). In other words, obedience to the presently applicable commandments should automatically result from our devotion to the LORD Jesus.

With the coming of the New Covenant, commandments have actually increased in number. There are approximately 1,050 in the New Testament. But the emphasis is no longer on just keeping commandments. Jesus shifted our attention upward to the "First Great Commandment" (loving God with all the heart, mind, soul and strength) and the second that is "like it" (loving our neighbor as ourselves). The Messiah insisted, "On these two commandments hang all the law and the prophets" (Matthew 22:40). If we teach our children this dual-emphasis in life—loving God and loving others—all other commandments should fall into place.

LORD GOD ALMIGHTY, I declare that we as a family are accountable to You. I submit to Your authority and believe in Your commandments. I trust in Your promise to write Your law within my heart—and I pray You will do the same for my child, that we may have a natural, inborn inclination to walk in Your ways. I pray that _____ will willingly embrace the "First Great Commandment" of loving God with all the heart, and the "Second Great Commandment" of loving others as we love ourselves. As these complementary attitudes take over his/her heart and life, keeping the rest of Your commandments will automatically ensue. I pass this knowledge to my son/daughter believing that _____ will have a passion to live within Your revealed will for humankind—in Jesus' Name, Amen (Let it be so)!

54 *Mature Plants*

*Rescue me and deliver me from the hand of foreigners,
whose mouth speaks lying words, and whose right hand is a
right hand of falsehood—
    That our sons may be as plants grown up in their youth;
that our daughters may be as pillars, sculptured in palace style.*
(Psalms 144:11-12)

This is a parent's prayerful plea to be delivered from the deceitful influence of the ungodly, in order to be a good role model. Children normally imitate their parents. If we succeed in bearing fruit for the Kingdom, they have a greater potential of doing the same. Both sons and daughters become as "plants grown up in their youth"—in other words, having been "planted" in the truth at an early age, they tend to mature spiritually at a more rapid rate.

Timothy was a pastor in the early church, and was, apparently, quite young. We assume this, because Paul urged him, "Let no one despise your youth" (1 Timothy 4:12). He must have developed in God quickly, because "from childhood" he knew "the holy Scriptures" (2 Timothy 3:15). "Genuine faith" was evidenced in him, for it first resided in his grandmother Lois, then his mother, Eunice. It was part of a wonderful legacy passed to him.

I have witnessed this many times in ministry-minded families. There is no greater modern-day example than Pastor Tommy Barnett, a greatly admired friend who started preaching in his teens. He watched his own father minister to the poor and downtrodden for years in Kansas City. He admits, *"Some things are taught; some are caught. I really caught my 'giving-ness' from my dad."*[†] Now Pastor Tommy has passed the torch to his sons who also "caught it" and grew into "mature plants" at an early age. Matthew Barnett pastors the "Dream Center" in Los Angeles, an incredible church that has become a model worldwide for 24/7 ministry to the poor. May your child also "catch it" and become a "mature plant" at an early age.

LORD GOD, help me to walk in "genuine faith," then reproduce the same in my son/daughter. I have "planted" _____ "in the house of the LORD." Therefore, I expect him/her to "flourish" in the things of God. Awaken in my child the understanding that earthly things are temporary and heavenly things are eternal— and give him/her a desire for those things which endure forever. I confess that _____ will mature in God at an early age. Even as Hannah "planted" her son, Samuel, in God's house and he became a "mature plant" early in life—receiving supernatural visitations as a child—so let it be for my son/daughter—in Jesus' Name, Amen (Let it be so)! (Psalms 92:13)

† Tommy Barnett, *Hidden Power* (Charisma House, Lake Mary, FL, 2002) p. 40-41

55 Pillars of Truth

That our sons may be as plants grown up in their youth;
that our daughters may be as pillars, sculptured in palace style.
(Psalms 144:12)

Pillars are commonly used to symbolize inspiring traits like strength, wisdom, uprightness, unchangeableness, authority, excellence and resolve—characteristics that make good leaders. It takes pillar-like believers to successfully "uphold" God's work in this world, not flimsy spiritual props that give way under pressure. Though he was but a child, God told Jeremiah that He would make him like "an iron pillar"—immovable in the face of opposition (Jeremiah 1:18).

The church as a whole is described as a "pillar...of the truth" (1 Timothy 3:15 MKJV). So every member of the church—adult or child—should exhibit "pillar-like" qualities and fill the role of world-changers and history-makers. Such persons have a divine design for their lives, that stretches from time to eternity. By the King of king's decree, they are "sculptured in palace style"—supportive columns of the government of God in the Kingdom which is yet to come. (See Revelation 3:12.)

PRAYER/CONFESSION

LORD GOD, thank You for making my son/daughter like a pillar—
unmovable, unshakable and unchanging in his/her commitment
to You—strong, wise, upright, full of authority, determined and
excellent in all things. I pray that _____ will be like
Jeremiah, standing for the truth—like an iron pillar—even when
it is unpopular. Finally, I confess by faith that _____ will
ultimately be like a pillar "sculptured in palace style"—an eternal
pillar in the temple of God—resurrected in perfection—one of those
who will rule with God over all things in the Kingdom which
is yet to come—in Jesus' Name, Amen (Let it be so)!

56 Polished Cornerstones

> *Rid me, and deliver me from the hand of strange children, whose mouth speaketh vanity, and their right hand is a right hand of falsehood:*
>
> *That our sons may be as plants grown up in their youth; that our daughters may be as corner stones, polished after the similitude of a palace.* (Psalms 144:11-12 KJV)

The King James Version of Psalm 144:12 describes the daughters of God's people as cornerstones, not pillars. A cornerstone is the beginning of a structure to which the rest of the building conforms—in style, size, slant and shape. This symbol speaks especially of those who are used of God to initiate unique purposes in the earth.

The most dominant example is the LORD Jesus Himself, referred to as the "Chief Cornerstone" in Ephesians 2:20. He was the initial Stone of a spiritual building that God began erecting in the earth nearly two thousand years ago—in order to inhabit it with His glory. The "construction" of this living cathedral, spanning two millennia, was definitely a new approach, a new revelation—something the Bible calls a "New Covenant" (Jeremiah 31:31).

If Jesus was the "Chief Cornerstone"—and his sons and daughters bear His image—believers should ALL fill the role of lesser "cornerstones"—called to be initiators, innovators, visionaries, purpose-driven people, history-makers and world-changers, people used of God to start new trends, so His divine designs can be fulfilled. Saying these things is not presumptuous or preposterous, for we are all "His workmanship, created in Christ Jesus for good works, which God prepared beforehand that we should walk in them" (Ephesians 2:10). We all have a purpose. We can all "begin" something of great value—even if on a small scale.

LORD GOD, I pray that You will give my son/daughter the courage to be an individual, to stand for what is right, and to be creative in serving You day by day. I confess that you will initiate something of great value through _____ that the world might be a better place. Empower him/her to be a "cornerstone," a trendsetter: establishing divinely inspired plans and purposes in the earth. Give me grace to prepare my child, not for the "shack" of mediocrity, but the "palace" of excellence, polishing _____ so that his/her gifts and callings are fully manifested— in Jesus' Name, Amen (Let it be so).

57 A Good Life

"I will give them singleness of heart and singleness of
purpose, so that they will fear Me forever—this will be for
their own good and for the good of their children after them."
(Jeremiah 32:39 CJB)

Never compromising, never accepting defeat, never wavering
from God's perfect will—this is "singleness of heart"—and this is
how we are called to live. This passage foretells two "good" things
that will happen. Number one: it will result in a "good life" for any
parent—a life that is full of purpose, full of peace and full of fruit.
Number two: it becomes a pattern for our children to follow. By
living out the "good life" before them (and reaping its benefits), we
awaken in them the knowledge and desire to follow in our footsteps.

Of course, you might be whispering, "Reality check—that all
sounds real nice, but I haven't been consistent. I haven't stayed
focused." It is never too late to start over. God loves to forget the past
and grant new beginnings. It helps to see this promise was originally
given to a generation that miserably failed God. Defeated by the
Babylonians, they lost everything and were carried away as slaves.
But God promised they would be restored to their homeland. If they
could pick up the pieces and start again, so can you. (See Psalms
27:13.)

PRAYER/CONFESSION

LORD GOD, first, I repent of any inconsistencies that have been in
my life. Forgive me for those times I've failed as a parent to model
a Christ-like walk before my child. I pray You will grant me
"singleness of heart" and "singleness of purpose"—that I may never
depart from the things of God. I pray this unwavering determination
will also be awakened in _____ so that both of us can truly
experience "a good life" filled with the goodness of the LORD—
in Jesus' Name, Amen (Let it be so).

58 The Glory of God

Let Your work appear to Your servants, and Your glory
to their children.   (Psalms 90:16)

Moses wrote Psalm 90 by the influence of the Holy Spirit. We know this, because—"All scripture is given by the inspiration of God" (2 Timothy 3:16). The word "inspiration" means *to breath into.* So this was much more than just a prophet interceding for nation of Israel. It was the Holy Spirit, "breathing" into that prophet a petition concerning all God's people of every era.

Whenever the Holy Spirit prays, the Father answers—without a doubt. So according to this inspired prayer—if we are truly "servants" of God, we can fully expect to see God work in our lives and manifest His glory to our children.

Primarily, the glory of the LORD is His manifested presence (as happened on Mount Sinai, in the Temple of Solomon, and the Upper Room). It also speaks of demonstrations of His power that bring honor and praise to His Name. The Holy Spirit has already interceded these things over our children through Moses. It is our responsibility to believe, confess and praise God for the fulfillment of this divine design.

PRAYER/CONFESSION

LORD GOD, I declare that I am a servant of God. I renew my commitment to serve Your purposes in this world. Because I am yielded this way, I expect You to work in my life and I expect to participate in Your works in this world. I also confess, by faith in this promise, that Your glory will be manifested to my son/daughter. I praise You for supernaturally revealing your power and your greatness to _____ *that praise might flow from his/her life upward to Your throne. LORD, I trust You to do glorious things—in my child, for my child and through my child—that will bring glory to Your Name forevermore—Amen (Let it be so)!*

59 An Inheritance from the Lord

Children are an inheritance from the LORD. They are a reward from Him. (Psalms 127:3 GW)

All those who transfer an inheritance to their heirs do so several ways: the heritage of "what they have," "what they do"and the greater legacy (for those who are Christlike) of "who they are." According to our key verse, children are part of the inheritance God gives His people. God is the *Creator* (that's who He is) and one of His most wonderful abilities is *creativity* (that's what He does). So one of the greatest inheritance-gifts He can pass to us is *procreative* ability.

What a profound thing—that a man and woman can unite in marriage and impart their image and likeness to their offspring. Furthermore, when any child is conceived in the womb, it contains a soul with the capacity of living forever! God could have reserved this *creation* right to Himself, but He rejoiced to share with us a powerful reflection of who He is and what He does.

PRAYER/CONFESSION

LORD GOD, first I thank You for my child. I receive_____ as an inheritance from God. I praise You that my image and values are being passed to my son/daughter. I am a co-laborer with You, creatively working—both naturally and spiritually—to fill the earth with God-loving people. I thank You for the ability to transfer to my child an inheritance of "what I have," but more importantly, an inheritance of "who I am and what I do." I am a servant of God, a child of God, and a member of the bride of Christ, married to You forever. These glorious facets of my identity, by faith, I bequeath to _____ . May he/she receive this inheritance with gratitude and faith, and then become "an inheritance from the LORD" passed to the next generation—in Jesus' Name, Amen (Let it be so)!

60 God's Reward

Children are an inheritance from the LORD. They are a reward from Him. (Psalms 127:3 GW)

A reward is something given in return for good behavior or exceptional performance. According to Hebrews 11:6, those who come to God must first "believe that He is, and that He is a rewarder of those who diligently seek Him." This is the nature of God. He so enjoys compensating His offspring for their service that when the LORD returns, "His reward" will be "with Him" (Isaiah 62:11). Yet rewards are not just futuristic; God rewards us in this life as well.

In our key passage, God declares the "fruit of the womb is His reward" (KJV). So one way God rewards our commitment to Him is sending children into our lives. They are meant to bring joy, fulfillment and the perpetuation of our name and values. Unfortunately, for some believers, the opposite happens. For a season, their children bring sorrow and heartbreak; discarding their values and even rejecting their faith. Should parents in this situation succumb to depression and just give up? "No, a thousand times, No!" Instead, they need to reaffirm over and over—as we all should—that our children are truly a reward from God. Confessing this truth in faith has the power to turn any situation around.

PRAYER/CONFESSION

LORD GOD, I claim this passage by faith: that my child is part of the inheritance that You have given Me. _____ is a gift from God, sent into my life as a reward of my commitment to You. I confess and believe that he/she will fulfill the role You intended—bringing joy and fulfillment in my life, and that he/she will perpetuate Bibical values in the earth. I have planted many seeds of truth in _____ .
I believe that he/she will bear much fruit for the Kingdom and ultimately receive a great reward from God as well—
in Jesus' Name, Amen (Let it be so)!

61 A Real Blessing

Children are a gift from the Lord; they are a real blessing. (Psalms 127:3 TEV)

When God first appeared to Abraham, He promised, "I will bless you...and you will be a blessing...and in you all the families of the earth will be blessed" (Genesis 12:2-3). Later on He pledged, "in your seed shall all the nations of the earth be blessed" (Genesis 22:18). God promised to bless Abraham by giving him children, then God promised to use those children to bless all the families of the earth (racial or cultural groups) and every nation.

What a blessing it is to have children who bear your image, both naturally and spiritually! What a blessing to have them return your love! What a blessing to see them mature and fulfill their dreams! What an even greater blessing it is to see them bless others with the truth and expand God's blessing around the globe! I claim this status—of being a "real blessing"—for you and yours!

PRAYER/CONFESSION

LORD GOD, I know the Scripture announces that those who are "of faith" are "blessed with faithful Abraham." I declare that one of my greatest blessings will be the continuation of God's blessing through my offspring. I confess that _____ is, and will be, a great blessing to me, but more importantly, he/she will be a blessing to You and to many others during his/her sojourn in this world. May this blessing of God flow so powerfully through _____ that it ultimately extends around the globe in its influence —in Jesus' Name, Amen (Let it be so)! (Galatians 3:9)

62 Spiritual Weapons

Behold, children are a heritage from the LORD, the fruit of the womb is a reward.

Like arrows in the hand of a warrior, so are the children of one's youth.

Happy is the man who has his quiver full of them. They shall not be ashamed, but shall speak with their enemies in the gate. (Psalms 127:3-5)

"Arrows in the hand of a warrior"—what a peculiar way of describing the children of God-loving parents! Yet when we consider the global, spiritual war raging over the souls of all human beings, it makes sense that godly parents are truly "warriors." Good parents daily fight the good fight of faith against spiritual darkness, in their own lives and the lives of others.

Prayerful mothers and fathers often receive inspired insights concerning the giftings that rest upon their children. Their God-given responsibility is to "load" their sons and daughters in the "bow" of a life pulled "tight" with commitment, then "shoot" them toward their God-given destiny.

The more children you have—serving God and fulfilling His purpose—the greater your happiness. The Contemporary English Version of verse five explains, "The more you have, the better off you will be, because they will protect you when your enemies attack…" When you teach your children how to be "weapons of righteousness" in the hands of God, their duty is to come to your rescue in time of need (Romans 6:13 Mon).

PRAYER/CONFESSION

LORD GOD of hosts, You are a God of war. You are presently fighting evil principalities and powers for the control of this world. I declare that my son/daughter is not only an arrow in MY quiver. According to Isaiah 49:2, he/she is an arrow in YOUR quiver as well—a weapon in the hands of the Almighty God. Give me grace to know the target of my child's destiny, so that as Your representative, I can shoot _____ toward the "bull's eye" of the perfect will of God for his/her life. I pray that _____ will be used of God to win great spiritual battles, so that the Kingdom of God might advance in this world. Whenever the enemy tries to slip through an entrance ("a gate") into our family circle, let me be unashamed as a parent as I watch _____ oppose all satanic plots, defending "the gate" and conquering valiantly for the cause of Christ—in Jesus' Name, Amen (Let it be so)!

63 Chosen by God

"Out of heaven He let you hear His voice, that He might instruct you; on earth He showed you His great fire, and you heard His words out of the midst of the fire.

And because He loved your fathers, therefore He chose their descendants after them; and He brought you out of Egypt with His Presence, with His mighty power."

(Deuteronomy 4:36-37)

According to this passage, one of God's primary motivations for choosing the nation of Israel was simply His love for their forefathers: Abraham, Isaac and Jacob. In Deuteronomy 7:7, He added that He chose Israel because of the "oath which He swore" to the patriarchs—not because the Israelites were a great nation, for quite the contrary, they were the "least of all peoples."

God's personality has not changed. True Christians are deeply loved of God, just as the patriarchs were. Therefore, it is believable that He will treat their offspring in a similar way—acknowledging them as His "special treasure" (Deuteronomy 7:6). Of course, in the New Covenant, God has opened His heart and His arms to the entire human race, and not just one particular nation or people-group. However, the offspring of the righteous are still very important to Him.

PRAYER/CONFESSION

LORD GOD, I love You with all of my heart. I am convinced that You also love me with an everlasting love, and nothing can separate me from Your love. You have surrounded my family with wonderful promises. Because of the bond of love between You and me, I believe that You will choose my child as Your special treasure; leading, instructing, blessing and helping _____ in numerous ways, that he/she might fulfill Your purposes, for time and eternity—in Jesus' Name, Amen (Let it be so)!

64 Everlasting Life

"For as the new heavens and the new earth which I will make shall remain before Me," says the LORD, "So shall your descendants and your name remain." (Isaiah 66:22)

There is no greater pledge from the lips of God than this: that our offspring will abide in His presence forever. According to this verse, such an expectation is just as stable, permanent and unchanging as the New Creation. God longs for a restored universe, free from evil, permeated with peace and immersed in His infinite love. More than that, He longs for the day when both we and our descendants are transformed fully into His image—perfected and glorified—shining like the sun in the Kingdom of our Father.

Does this mean that our children will live on eternally in a flawless, heavenly state, whether they personally choose to serve God or not? Certainly not! However, it does mean that the Father will honor our commitment to Him by extending extraordinary grace to our children in enabling them to make the right choices. He will go beyond the norm in helping them to follow the path that leads to an infinite inheritance.

When the judgment of Sodom and Gomorrah was about to transpire, the Bible explains, "God remembered Abraham" and "saved Lot from the terrible destruction" (Genesis 19:29 KJV, CEV). Although Lot was just Abraham's nephew, he and his family escaped the torrent of fiery brimstone that fell—just because of the family tie they shared. How much more will God do this kind of thing for the children of His people! We must believe this enough to thank God in advance, claiming 1 John 2:25 for the whole family—"This is the promise that He has promised *us*—eternal life" (1 John 2:25, emphasis by author).

LORD GOD, I believe that my child's eternal destiny is secure with You. In all of his/her struggles in life, I believe You will remember my commitment to You and save _____ from this destructive world. You are the Almighty and the intentions of Your heart will be fulfilled. You intend to bring forth a New Creation, free from darkness, free from pain, free from evil, free from satanic influence and free from the curse. Nothing will change this divine purpose or prevent it from coming to pass. In like manner, I believe that You intend to grant _____ the grace to love You, to serve You and to abide in Your presence forever. I confess that _____ will also be free from darkness, free from pain, free from evil, free from satanic influence and free forever from the curse. As the New Creation shall remain before You—filled with Your presence and made perfect in every way—so shall my offspring remain: perfected in God irreversibly and everlastingly— in Jesus' Name, Amen (Let it be so)!

65 *Revelation*

"The secret things belong to the Lord our God, but those things which are revealed belong to us and to our children forever, that we may do all the words of this law."

(Deuteronomy 29:29)

There are some mysteries—"secret things"—concerning God, the universe and humanity that we may never comprehend in this life. But there are revealed truths that we can count among our most precious possessions. When God reveals truth, it changes us permanently, that we might then become truth's means of changing the world around us. There are many Biblical examples of key "revelations" that brought about great personal, national and even global transformations:

- God revealed Himself to Noah and the human race was saved from extinction.
- God revealed Himself to Abraham and a covenant nation was born.
- God revealed Himself to Moses and Israel was delivered from slavery.
- God revealed Himself to Saul (later to be named Paul) and the door to the Gentiles swung open wide.

Now God has revealed Himself to you in a very special way. He has opened your understanding concerning the 65 things He pledges to do for the children of the righteous. This revelation belongs to YOU and to YOUR CHILD, and nothing can steal it from you. Go ahead! Expect results just as dramatic, on a personal level, as the building of the ark, the miracle birth of Isaac, the collapse of the Egyptian empire and the Gospel spreading to every nation. If "revealed truth" could accomplish such great feats of faith for others, just what will it accomplish for you and your child? Start praising God now for the miracle that you need.

PRAYER/CONFESSION

LORD GOD, I thank You for all the revelations You have given me, especially this revelation of the promises You have bestowed on the children of Your people. This insight belongs to me. I claim it as a gift from God. It belongs to my child _____ also. Nothing can steal it from us. It is part of the wonderful inheritance that You have imparted to us. This awesome truth has come into our home to bless, to change and to transform us, that we might bring blessing, change and transformation to the world. I pray and believe that You will activate these promises in our behalf, LORD, but more than that—I believe You will use us to activate these promises in the lives of others. I declare that this blessing will not end with us; it will keep passing from one life to another until it encircles the globe—in Jesus' Name, Amen (Let it be so)!

PART THREE

Final Thoughts

"More things are wrought by prayer than this world dreams of. Wherefore, let thy voice rise like a fountain, night and day." —ALFRED LORD TENNYSON

"There is always a moment in childhood when the door opens and lets the future in."

—Graham Green

The Coat of Many Colors

Now faith is the substance of things hoped for, the evidence of things not seen. (Hebrews 11:1)

By now your faith should be soaring. It really is true. God gave these promises and He intends to keep them. Certainly, at this point, you have already believed, confessed, wept over, shouted about, and even committed to memory many of these divine pledges.

Just as Jacob made his favored son, Joseph, a coat of many colors, and placed it upon him—so you have spiritually woven a rainbow-colored garment of 65 promises and lovingly placed it upon your son or your daughter. What a powerful thing you have done! What a pivotal point in your relationship! What an impartation of favor—from God and from you!

The original "coat of many colors" was symbolic of Joseph's calling from God—His anointing—that invisible "covering" from the heavenly Father that propelled him mightily and successfully through all the challenging circumstances he faced in life—first, rejection and betrayal, then enslavement, then finally, false accusation and imprisonment in Pharaoh's dungeon. Against all odds this "spiritual garment" took him from the bottom to the top in one day, when Pharaoh appointed him prime minister over all the land of Egypt.

Let it be so for your child as well! May these promises be a "garment of favor" that propels your son or daughter through every challenge in life into the glorious destiny and divine purpose that yet awaits in the future.

A Rainbow of Promise

"Children rarely experience breakthroughs on their own.
Left alone, few will travel quickly down the road to their
potential. They need their parents to help them along."
—JOHN C. MAXWELL[†]

It has already been sufficiently proven that God's blessing passes down the family line from consecrated foreparents—for "He remembers His covenant forever, the Word which He commanded, for *a thousand generations*" (Psalms 105:8, emphasis by author).

The length of a "generation" is not exactly defined in Scripture. It could be anywhere from 20 to 100 years (probably 40 years— see Psalm 95:10). Whatever figure you choose, multiply it by a thousand and you've got a huge stretch of time, somewhere between 20,000 and 100,000 years. How powerful it is that your walk with God could have such a lingering influence! And if the "overflow" of your relationship with God can persist that far into the future— long after you are gone and your name, forgotten—how much more will it bring God's power and blessing upon those generations immediately following you, while you are still alive to witness God's faithfulness! This is a powerful truth—but it gets even better.

Let's examine God's pledge to Noah. After this great patriarch and his family were kept safe for about a year in the ark, the floodwaters subsided. Then God brought them out to see an awesome sight: the first, spectacular, color-filled rainbow stretching across the sky. The Most High explained to Noah the reason behind such an impressive display of divine artistry:

> *"... This is the sign of the covenant which I make between*
> *Me and you, and every living creature that is with you, for*
> *perpetual generations:*
> *I set My rainbow in the cloud, and it shall be for the*
> *sign of the covenant between Me and the earth.*

It shall be, when I bring a cloud over the earth, that the rainbow shall be seen in the cloud;

And I will remember My covenant which is between Me and you and every living creature of all flesh; the waters shall never again become a flood to destroy all flesh."

(Genesis 9:12-15)

Not only was this a covenant promise to Noah; it was a covenant promise to all his seed—*for perpetual generations.* Here we are, millenniums later, yet every human being alive in this world (righteous or wicked) is a recipient of this covenant commitment, and can trust that it will be kept. The earth will never be submerged again. Period.

Why not expect something just as powerful and long-lasting in God's commitment to you? Noah's God is your God. His nature is the same; His ways have not changed. He may give you a sign too (if you ask Him) of His dedication to your family. (It's Biblical. See Isaiah 7:11.) Know that your relationship with God has positioned all of your offspring under a spiritual kind of rainbow, an arc of hope, a multi-colored band of 65 divine pledges. These promises will remain "living and powerful," hovering over them—*"for perpetual generations"* (Hebrews 4:12, Genesis 9:12). That stretches into the future with a never-ending influence, an even greater pledge than the "thousand generation" commitment of Psalm 105:8.

So quit allowing fear to cloud your view. Stop being apprehensive and worried—picturing your offspring as weak, vulnerable, impressionable, beset by the world, wearing the rags of carnality, or buffeted by the storms of life. Instead "see" your seed standing strong, confident, unafraid and blessed of heaven—each one wearing a "coat of many colors" (the sign of God's favor: a treasured, family heirloom that can be traced back to you)—and each one abiding under a "rainbow of promise" (a covenant sign of God's power to bring you and your offspring out of every storm).

Oh! Remember one more thing—WYSIWYG!

What does that mean?

It's an acronym—one I hope you will never forget.

W — what

Y — you

S — say

I — is

W — what

Y — you

G — get

So don't just "see" this condition for your seed.

"Say it"—as often as you can. ("My child is clothed in a spiritual 'coat of many colors'; my child abides under a 'rainbow of promise' that stretches from the beginning to the end of his/her life.") The more you say it, the more you will believe it. The more you believe it, the greater likelihood that you will see optimum spiritual conditions birthed by God in the lives of your offspring.

I urged you to embrace the power of confession in the beginning of this book. I cannot over-emphasize it, now that we are coming to the end. But let me <u>underscore</u> an important, additional piece of essential information: don't put your faith in some repetitious confession; put your faith in THE GREAT AND MIGHTY GOD who watches over His Word (as you confess it) to perform it in your behalf. And then abide in HOPE—which, by the way, gives us another great acronym—

H — having

O — only

P — positive

E — expectations.

---

†Maxwell, John, *Breakthrough Parenting* (Focus on the Family Pub., Colorado Springs, CO, 1996) p. 6.

Two Powerful Symbols

"...the Spirit uses things that are seen to teach us concerning the things which are unseen."
—WALTER LEWIS WILSON

Have you ever noticed the small, black boxes that Jewish men wear on their foreheads and upper arms, especially during prayer? These objects are called "frontlets" in the Old Testament and "phylacteries" in the New (Exodus 13:16, Matthew 23:5 — traditionally referred to also as "tefillin"). If you were to open one of these boxes, you would find either four strips of parchment in four chambers (the head tefillin) or one four-columned strip of parchment in one chamber (the arm tefillin). On the parchment are four hand-written passages of Scripture: Exodus 13:1-10, Exodus 13:11-16, Deuteronomy 6:4-9 and Deuteronomy 11:13-21. These passages reveal essential truths for God's people, especially the Israelites of old. You should read these references when you can, just to get a better understanding of this custom.

A related tradition is the mounting of something called a "mezuzah" on the gates and doorposts of Jewish homes. The mezuzah is a handwritten parchment housed in a small rectangular box, normally about 4 to 8 inches in length and about 1 to 2 inches in width. This ornamental container, which may be made of wood, metal, glass or ceramic, contains two of the four Bible passages found in the phylacteries: Deuteronomy 6:4-9 and Deuteronomy 11:13-21. When Jews enter their homes, they will normally touch or kiss the mezuzah as a worshipful sign—a reaffirmation, over and over, of the promises contained within—a belief that the God of Abraham is protecting their home, watching over their family and executing these promises in their behalf.

Four verses out of one of those key passages explain the purpose of these two related customs: the wearing of tefillin and the mounting of mezuzahs. The Most High, the King of the universe, commands:

*"Therefore you shall lay up these words of Mine in your heart and in your soul, and bind them as a **sign on your hand**, and they shall be as **frontlets between your eyes**.*

You shall teach them to your children, speaking of them when you sit in your house, when you walk by the way, when you lie down, and when you rise up.

*And you shall write them on the doorposts of your house and on your gates [the **mezuzah**],*

That your days and the days of your children may be multiplied in the land of which the LORD *swore to your fathers to give them, like the days of the heavens above the earth."* (Deuteronomy 11:18-21)

If you are Jewish, most likely, you already understand the spiritual, symbolic implications of these customs. If you are non-Jewish, you may be wondering how to relate to this information. Take it figuratively—and relate it to the insight contained within this book. You will probably never wear a frontlet on your forehead—but these 65 promises can dominate your thinking, until you are more convinced of these divine pledges than any negative circumstance you are facing with your child. Also, you will probably never literally wear a tefillin on your arm—but you can let the 65 promises of this book guide the relationship you have with your offspring. That's what the arm and hand symbolize—how you relate to, and interact with, others.

Concerning these two traditions (tefillin and mezuzahs), Ed Young points out, "The Deuteronomy passage lays out the principle of establishing an environment full of God's Word and truth. A family is to be saturated with the understanding of His principles."[†] Translating these practices into a New Covenant perspective, you might consider doing the following:

- **Write** *some of the promises you have studied on index cards and post them around your home, on your refrigerator, or at the entrance to your child's room, as a constant, daily reminder.*

- ***Touch and confess*** *these posted promises from time to time in a worshipful gesture toward God, praising Him for their fullfillment.*
- ***Speak*** *to your child about these promises. Without being overbearing, weave them into your conversations in creative ways—as often as you can.*

"That your days and the days of your children may be multiplied...like the days of the heavens above the earth."

Phylacteries are small leather boxes with long straps so worshippers can wear the boxes on their foreheads and on their arms. Inside the boxes are scripture passages from the Torah. A phylactery worn on the left arm is a reminder to keep God's law with all your heart. The one worn on the forehead is to remind the wearer to focus his concentration on the law.[*]

A **mezuzah** is a sacred parchment inscribed with passages from the Torah. It is placed in a protective case and hung on the door-posts of Jewish homes.[**]

[†] Young, Ed, *The 10 Commandments of Parenting* (Moody Publishers, Chicago, IL, 2004) p. 158.
[*] **Phylactery**—Artwork: Courtesy of Beck Archives, Special Collections, Penrose Library, University of Denver. 1-30-2008, www.penlib.du.jpg
[**] **Mezuzah**—Artwork: Used by permission, Eitan Rechtman, 1-30-2008, www.holyland-souvenirs.com

Under the Shadow of the Almighty

"God is truth and light His shadow." —PLATO

Always remember, because you are under God's authority—and your child is under your authority—there is an overflow of divine influence that passes through you into your offspring's life. You have clout in heaven; you have friends in high places. The Most High God honors your position as a parent. In Boaz-like manner, He casts His garment of spiritual authority over you—a redemptive cloak of protection, provision and power. That "covering" affects both you and your offspring. (See Ruth 3.)

One of my favorite Bible verses is Psalm 91:1, "He who dwells in the secret place of the Most High shall abide under the shadow of the Almighty." First, I want you to notice the two primary parts of this sentence: the first phrase presents God's mandate—that believers dwell in His secret place (a "place" of communion and commitment). The second phrase presents His promised response—that He will overshadow us all the days of our lives.

Consider the two names of God revealed in this verse. This divine commitment is made to individuals who dwell in "the secret place of the *Most High*" (Hebrew-*El Elyon*)—in other words, those who acknowledge God as *the Most High* in their lives—*higher* than anything or anyone else. Such devoted persons are then privileged to "abide under the shadow of *the Almighty*" (Hebrew-*El Shaddai*)—under the covering of His all-sufficient protection, provision and power.

Don't forget, your offspring also come under this same "overshadowing Promise" by default. Because of your walk with God, this invisible, spiritual canopy spreads over their earthly existences, with very visible results.

One of my most vivid childhood memories illustrates this truth wonderfully. Back in the latter 1950s, my mother, and all four children (my brother, Bob, and two sisters, Winnie and Betty) were flying back to Guantanamo Bay, Cuba, where my father was stationed. Unknown to us, right when the plane landed in Santiago, Castro and his forces were descending upon the city to seize it. The airport was shut down, so we were not able to get our flight out.

That night was a very frightful experience for a six-year-old. We were escorted to a motel room (dingy and dirty, but a great comfort nonetheless). There was no sleeping. Guns were cracking and bullets flying as the rebels streamed through the alleys and streets. All of us huddled together, lying down on the grimy floor. Mom explained that in that position, any bullets passing through the walls or window of the room would be less likely to hit us.

My father soon found out about our dilemma. Hurriedly, he obtained an official car from the Naval Base with an American flag flying from the antenna. He dressed up in the full military regalia provided to him as a Commander in the U.S. Navy, with all his medals and stripes. Driving over treacherous mountain roads, he rushed to get where his family was "hunkered down." He made it past all the roadblocks and stakeouts. When they realized who he was, the insurgents just waved him on. No problem.

Once in the car, he told all of us children to crouch down on the floorboard between the front and back seats. To this day, I remember looking up in awe at the stream of soldiers marching by with rifles held to their shoulders. Most of them kept their eyes straight ahead, as if they were oblivious to us. I didn't fully understand why, I just knew that once my father got there, we were safe. When the rebel soldiers stared at the car, their gaze tended to shift toward the red, white and blue flag—the stars and stripes— that identified our citizenship.

Their immediate assumption must have been the untouchable status of those riding in the vehicle. Because my father was submitted to the authority of the chain of command above him, there was a transfer of authority down to him—from the President of the United States and his cabinet, to the Congress and the Senate, to the Pentagon and the Joint Chiefs of Staff, all the way to this one Naval Commander, Andrew Shreve, passing through enemy territory all by himself.

Yet he wasn't really "by himself." There was an invisible host behind him—multiplied thousands of men and women, the entire governmental, judicial, law enforcement and military structure of the United States of America. The guerillas knew if they harmed or injured us in any way, they might be inviting a united response from all of these—something, at that point, they were not prepared to face. So because my father was under the "shadow" of the United States government, he was safe—and because we were under our father's "shadow," we were safe.

So it is for you and your children. At this point, your offspring may even be behind enemy lines. But go after them, just like my father did. Put on your "military garments": the whole armor of God. Fly the bloodstained banner of Calvary on the "antenna" of your prayer life, and bring them back home. You are not alone. The LORD of hosts, the God of an army of angels, has sent forth His ministering spirits to watch over you and your offspring. You are under God's shadow, and they are under yours.

Believe this with all of your heart.
Believe this with all of your mind.
Believe this with all of your might.
Your faith will make the difference.

A miracle is already in motion—for you and your family.

Let it be so—for the Glory of God and the Praise of His Name!

Promise Scriptures in Biblical Order

In this book, the promises are not placed in the order in which they appear in Scripture. Just in case you would like that information, it is included here. The following passages are not only the 65 promise scriptures; a few verses have been taken from the commentaries and explanations.

All Scripture passages are from the NKJV unless otherwise noted.

The Promises in Alphabetical Order

PART FOUR

Praise & Progress Journal

Praise Reports

_____

_____

_____

_____

_____

_____

_____

_____

_____

_____

_____

_____

_____

_____

_____

_____

_____

_____

_____

_____

_____

_____

_____

_____

_____

_____

_____

_____

_____

Personal Prayers

Personal Confessions

Memorable Happenings

Family Vision Statement

In Search of the True Light

An in-depth comparison of over 20 world religions

by Mike Shreve

In 1970 Mike Shreve was a teacher of Kundalini Yoga at four universities, and ran a yoga ashram in Tampa, Florida. After receiving a supernatural encounter with the Lord Jesus Christ, his heart, life and belief system were all dramatically changed. In this book he shares his own personal, spiritual journey and compares the beliefs of over 20 religions in seven basic doctrinal areas (something he terms "the seven pillars of wisdom"). Both commonalities and contradictions are revealed. He also responds to concepts like reincarnation, karma, monism and pantheism, from a Biblical perspective. This one-of-a-kind book will be a great addition to your library! It is a perfect gift for those who are involved in far eastern religions seeking ultimate truth.

ISBN: 978-0-942507-73-7   **—Price 19.99**

"This is a great book to give to a non-Christian searching for the truth."   —Kerby Anderson, Point of View Radio Program

"In Search Of The True Light is a classic...I have not been able to put down this book."   —Pastor Matthew Barnett, The Dream Center

"An incredible research project..."
—C. Peter Wagner, Founder of Global Harvest Industries

A portrait of Mike Shreve as a yoga teacher in 1970 and a present day picture.

MIKE SHREVE, B.Th.,D.D., has been teaching God's Word since 1971. He is the author of nine books and three Bible studies, the founder of "Deeper Revelation Books," and the visionary behind "The True Light Project," an outreach to followers of non-Christian worldviews.

www.thetruelight.net

Our Glorious Inheritance

The Revelation of the Titles of the Children of God

Volume Three

by Mike Shreve

The "OUR GLORIOUS INHERITANCE" eight volume series explores a powerful and edifying subject in God's Word: the revelation of over 1,000 names and titles God has given His people. Each name gives unique insight into a certain aspect of the total inheritance available to sons and daughters of God. Seeing the revelation of ALL of our names and titles provides the most comprehensive and complete view of our spiritual identity—who we are and what we possess as children of God.

In Volume Three, over 150 inspiring names for God's people are explored, including: *the Anointed of the Lord, the Blessed of the Father, Children of the Kingdom, Heirs of the Kingdom, Good Ground, Good Seed, Good Soldiers, the Just, Peacemakers, the Poor in Spirit* and *Trees of Righteousness*. Get ready for a transformational experience!

ISBN: 978-0-942507-54-6   **—Price: $17.95**

The following endorsements were given concerning Volume One of this book series—

"As I read these wonderful titles and nodded in understanding...I realized...who I am in Christ."
— Jamie Buckingham, Former Editor of *Charisma* Magazine

"In addition to challenging the Christian leader in his or her way with God, the text will serve as excellent reference material. Scripture abounds and pastors will love Shreve's categorizing and indexing."   *—Ministries Today*

"Our Glorious Inheritance by Mike Shreve contains 'hidden treasure' about our inheritance as children of God. Shreve discovers...Biblical titles that reveal our rank in the universal plan of God...This book gives rich insight on God's attitude toward His children.
— Brian Peterson, *Charisma* Magazine

God's Strategy for Tragedy

A Documented Modern-day Miracle

by Ben Godwin

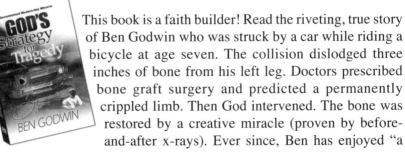

This book is a faith builder! Read the riveting, true story of Ben Godwin who was struck by a car while riding a bicycle at age seven. The collision dislodged three inches of bone from his left leg. Doctors prescribed bone graft surgery and predicted a permanently crippled limb. Then God intervened. The bone was restored by a creative miracle (proven by before-and-after x-rays). Ever since, Ben has enjoyed "a miracle walk on a miracle leg, serving in a miracle ministry."

- Do miracles still happen today?
- Why does God allow tragedy?
- How should we respond to tragedy?
- How can you receive a miracle?

This book provides solid answers to these and other questions and illustrates, both from the Scriptures and real life, how God can turn tragedy into a testimony.

ISBN: 978-0-942507-45-4   **—Price: $14.99**

BEN GODWIN, B.Th., began preaching at age thirteen and has been in full-time ministry since 1987. He presently serves as pastor of the Goodsprings Full Gospel Church near Birmingham, Alabama, and hosts a weekly television program called "The Word Workshop." Ben and his wife, Michelle, work as a team in ministry. They and their three children, Nathan, Emily and Noah reside in Goodspring, Alabama.

www.bengodwin.org

Authentic Enlightenment

The inspirational story of a spiritual seeker

by Vail Carruth

Transcendental Meditation still attracts many seekers to its beliefs and practices. Vail Carruth was one of the 'originals', joining this group shortly after its introduction in the U.S. In *Authentic Enlightenment* she candidly explains why she was drawn to TM in the early 60s and how she advanced to the point of becoming a certified teacher.

Referred to as a "scientific relaxation technique," TM seemed to bring some benefits. However, this yoga discipline primarily served to turn Vail inward. Though it calmed the senses and opened her to supernatural experiences, still there was something missing. She finally concluded that these techniques would never be able to fill the emptiness of her heart or satisfy her thirst for God.

Vail's spiritual journey took a new direction when she called upon the Name above all names—the Name of JESUS. It was only then that she experienced the reality of the HOLY SPIRIT and the unspeakable joy and fullness of GOD'S LOVE. Read her story and you, too, will be guided into transformation and wholeness in your life.

ISBN: 978-0-942507-42-3   **—Price: $15.95**

VAIL CARRUTH holds a BA in Fine Art from the University of California, Berkeley and studied piano at the San Francisco Conservatory of Music. She is a former teacher of TM who shares her experiences in the movement with diverse audiences, and why she shifted to a Biblical belief system. Vail is also an artist, even in the delightful way she paints a picture with her words. Her sole desire is to exalt her Creator and to make Him known to others.

www.living-light.net

Raised from the Dead

A True Account

by Richard L. Madison

After a horrible car accident, Richard Madison was pronounced dead-on-arrival at the hospital. His family was told three times to make funeral arrangements. God revealed Himself to Richard through an out-of-body experience, and ten weeks later he walked out of a wheelchair. He is now a walking miracle testimony to thousands of people throughout the world that God's love can powerfully restore even the most hopeless lives. This amazing book will build your faith.

ISBN: 978-0-942507-43-0 **—Price: $13.95**

"Jesus walked into that hospital room, and laid His hand on Rick Madison's head and healed Him." —Pat Robertson

"Fast living led to a dead end, but a new life began with an out-of-body experience." —Ben Kinchlow

"Richard, you've had everything go wrong that could go wrong and...you are a living miracle."
—Dr. Kenneth Sharp, Vanderbilt University Medical Center

⟫◆⟪

RICHARD MADISON is a full-time evangelist who travels the world to tell the remarkable story of how God raised him from the dead and completely delivered him from drugs and alcohol. Richard is a highly sought after speaker with a powerful healing and prophetic ministry. He and his family live in Oakman, Alabama.

www.rickmadison.org

Ordering Information

For a listing of other available books
please visit our website:

www.deeperrevelationbooks.org

or call: 1-423-478-2843

Wholesalers and retailers should contact Anchor Distributors
or Baker & Taylor Distributors at their respective websites:

www.anchordistributors.com

www.btol.com

Individuals desiring these books should send the amount
below, plus $5.00 s/h per book to:

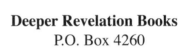

Deeper Revelation Books
P.O. Box 4260
Cleveland, TN 37320-4260

Be sure to include your complete shipping information
(P.O. Box or street address, etc.).

Discounts may be available for large quantities.

	QTY	PRICE	AMOUNT
GOD'S PROMISES FOR YOUR CHILDREN		$14.99	
IN SEARCH OF THE TRUE LIGHT		$19.99	
OUR GLORIOUS INHERITANCE (VOL. THREE)		$17.95	
AUTHENTIC ENLIGHTENMENT		$15.95	
GOD'S STRATEGY FOR TRAGEDY		$14.99	
RAISED FROM THE DEAD		$13.95	
(Add $5.00 s/h per book)	TOTAL AMOUNT		